INTERPRETING
"THE VOICE OF THE CUSTOMER"

by

Dr. Jon Anton
Adjunct Professor
Purdue University
Center for Customer-Driven Quality

and

Kevin L. Childs
President and Chief Customer Officer
UCN, Inc.

Editor
John Chatterley
BenchmarkPortal, LLC

Business Navigation

Only two centuries ago, early explorers (adventurous business executives of those bygone days) were guided primarily with a compass and celestial navigation using reference points like the North Star. Today's busy executive also needs guidance systems with just-in-time business intelligence to navigate through the challenges of locating, recruiting, keeping, and growing profitable customers. The Anton Press provides this navigational system through practical, how-to-do-it books for the modern day business executive.

Copyright © 2007 (17-Sep-07)

ISBN: 978-0-9761109-2-7 June 2007

The Anton Press, Santa Maria, CA 93455
Used pursuant to license. All rights reserved.

Table of Contents

List of Figures

DEDICATION I

I dedicate this book to my
friend Joe Patrick Piliero for
his life of sacrifice, patience,
and love in caring for his
disabled son, Joey.

Dr. Jon Anton

DEDICATION II

I dedicate this book to
Alisa, Braiden, Brooke,
Bryson and BJ ...

Without question, they
are my life and
inspiration...

Kevin L. Childs

ACKNOWLEDGEMENTS I

I wish to acknowledge the following individuals who in whole or in part inspired me to co-author this book:

1. I wish to acknowledge the assistance and support of Professor Richard A. Feinberg of Purdue University who, over the past fifteen years, has facilitated my pursuit of academic and scientific adventures. Without Professor Feinberg, this book would not have been possible.

2. I also wish to acknowledge the important part of Joe Ordyna of the eBay Corporation who encourage me to pursue post-email survey design, fielding, analysis, and interpretation. It was his example of survey data processing and interpreting that caused me to discover the power of simply asking customers where things needed improvement. Joe practically invented the concept of "asking, interpreting, and acting" on customer feedback data. Without Joe, this book would not have been possible.

3. I also wish to acknowledge the important role of Anita Rockwell in being a critical part in the creation, design, and implementation of many of the concepts treated in our book. Certainly, one of Anita's many skills is to understand the decision-making information requirements of professionals that operate customer service call centers. Without Anita, this book would not have been possible.

Dr. Jon Anton

ACKNOWLEDGEMENTS II

Winston Churchill once said that writing a book is an adventure. "To begin with it is a toy and an amusement. Then it becomes a mistress, then it becomes a master, then it becomes a tyrant. The last phase is that just as you are about to be reconciled to your servitude, you kill the monster and fling him to the public."

While acknowledging my obvious debt to such a renowned figure as Dr. Jon, I owe an even greater debt to the employees of UCN, as they have moved our company from an organization that provided network services (long distance & data services) to the first company that provides core contact center application services from within the network.

Through their tireless effort, they make it possible for our customers to "ask, interpret and act" upon the needs of those they serve.

My journey of asking, interpreting and acting began in 1991, when as a young manager in the staffing business, I found most contact centers did not have what it takes to exceed the expectations of their customers, and at times their employees (one of most important customers a company may have).

Through the leadership of my Father, Les, who taught me family is what life is all about, my Uncle Devon, who taught me what hard work meant, Dick Reinhold and Steve Whitworth, who taught me how to have fun doing it, Joyce Russell, who taught me the principles of having the right team and people with you on the journey brings passion into the work and Paul Jarman, Ted Stern and the entire leadership team at UCN, who believed we could "act" in such a way that our company could reinvent itself into what it is today.

Action is the reinvention each individual, department and company will take as they understand what their customers need in order for them to become the company's future apostles.

Kevin L. Childs

FOREWORD

By

Paul Jarman
CEO
The UCN Corporation

In my role as the executive most responsible for the vision and direction of my company, I can say with confidence that the Jon Anton and Kevin Childs team of co-authors have written a very useful and compelling manuscript with their "Interpreting the Voice of the Customer" book.

I am an avid reader of books written for top executives, and therefore, my personal library is full of books addressing the obvious topics of leadership, finance, legal, human resources, competitive analysis, managing customer relationships, marketing, and many others. This book is very, very different in that it treats the all-important topic of understanding customer feedback, a topic often lost to top executives who are too busy working on change initiatives that are not customer-driven.

What Anton and Childs have accomplished is to distinguish between the "feels good" nature of most customer survey initiatives, and the much more complex steps of interpreting the voice of the customer, and, most importantly "acting" upon the findings.

In my humble opinion, this book proves, without the slightest doubt, that companies that listen and act on customer feedback most often have the best products, with the most wanted features, sold at just the right price to gain market share, plus achieve maximum profit margins, and the best earnings per share.

The companies studied proved unequivocally that listening to your design engineers almost never makes you the winning company in your competitive space. Many companies consider themselves, with pride, to be engineering-driven. Unfortunately, engineering-driven companies often launch highly sophisticated products with incredible features, which unfortunately the customer does not want.

As one popular automobile manufacturer was quoted as saying, "we spend a lot of money running comprehensive statistics on solicited customer feedback. We don't ask our engineers what they think needs improving for next year's model, instead, we interpret the voice of our customers, and whatever comes out on top, we "tell" our engineers to create those features for next year's model. If the customer feedback indicated, without a doubt, that customers wanted a "fifth wheel" on next year's model automobile, we would instruct the engineers to do just that."

So the message of this book is "loud and clear," namely interpret customer feedback using the best available statistics, and then use this information to improve both your product and your services.

It seems almost trite and trivial that CEOs need to "hear" clearly what the majority of their customers want. Often we're too busy driving our companies simply "looking at the financial data"....meaning we're literally trying to drive while only looking through the rear-view mirror.

Anton and Childs have packed this book with real-world examples of:

1. how to ask the customer for feedback in real-time,

2. how to take customer feedback data, and process it into a form that can be easily interpreted by C-level executives,

3. and, finally and most importantly, how to take the interpreted data and take action to make changes based on a statistical interpretation of the voice of the customer.

I strongly suggest that you get a copy of this book and then make sure that you and your direct reports read the book, cover to cover. It is a "quick read." During your next business trip, you'll finish it on the airplane. Then begin a systematic application of its principles in order to make your company more "customer-driven" and profitable. The authors have a simple mantra for you and your customer relationship management strategy, namely:

Ask – Interpret - Act

CHAPTER 1: INTRODUCTION TO CUSTOMER FEEDBACK ANALYTICS

The Goals of Customer Feedback

Ask, Interpret, and Act are the steps in any customer feedback system, but the most important of these is ACT. Many, many companies spend thousands of dollars "asking" the customer "are you satisfied" through surveys. Very few companies have the resources and/or skill sets to "Interpret" the results that come in from these surveys. And, hardly any companies actually "Act" on the results. The sole purpose of this book is to help companies to achieve the real goal of customer feedback, and that is ACTION as dictated by the customer.

The authors want to point out that this book is a sequel to the popular book entitled "Listening to the Voice of the Customer." The important statistical techniques presented in the "Listening" book are not repeated here, but are frequently referenced. Therefore, for a complete picture of the "whole story" of survey analytics, we recommend that you refer to our Listening book for detailed statistical techniques.

Even a casual glance at business journals and business sections of daily newspapers reveals that the subject of customer satisfaction is receiving extraordinary attention. As markets shrink, companies scramble to keep their customers rather than expending greater and greater sums chasing fewer and fewer potential new customers.

The simple fact that it costs five to eight times as much to get new customers as it does to hold onto old ones is key to understanding the corporate drive to manage customer value by measuring and interpreting customer feedback.

1

A recent study by the authors' show that Chief Executives typical focus on the following six issues (in order of importance) in approving capital expenditures for new initiatives:

- cost reductions;

- revenue increases;

- customer satisfaction improvements;

- increases in market share;

- increases in wallet share;

- and, finally, scalability of the initiative.

It is interesting the emphasis all CEO place on measurement, for instance, Meg Whitman, President and CEO of eBay show us her value system by the figure that follows:

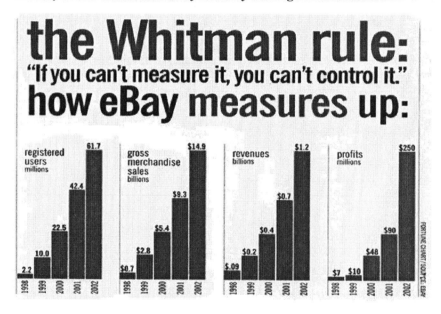

Figure 1: The Whitman Rule: "If you can't measure it, you can't control it". (Purdue Research Foundation)

2

Although "Customer Satisfaction" may no longer be a new buzzword in the business community, there is still an enormous gap between the stated goal of many companies to increase customer satisfaction and any attempts to implement that goal. For example, an analysis of the annual reports of all publicly owned companies listed in the Fortune 500 was undertaken by the Center for Customer-Driven Quality at Purdue University. That analysis failed to find any firms reporting the actual numbers of loyal and satisfied customers they serve, much less satisfaction trends among their customers.

While 87% of the 500 companies with annual revenues in excess of $100 million listed customer satisfaction as one of their most important corporate initiatives, we found that only 16.1% of the companies had any method in place to measure their effectiveness in satisfying the customer. This disparity clearly seems less a matter of corporate hypocrisy than a simple lack of information. Of the 365 companies that did not have a method in place, 336, or 92%, asked us for more information about measuring customer satisfaction.

Though many contact center managers measure customer satisfaction in some rudimentary way, see the figure that follows:

"Do You Collect Caller Opinions?"

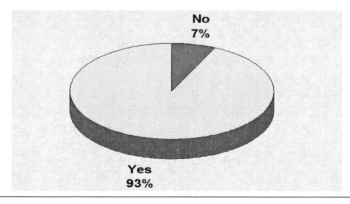

Figure 2: Many collect caller feedback. (Purdue Research Foundation)

But as can be seen from the next figure, few take the next steps.

"Do You Use the Caller Opinions to Influence Internal Change in Your Call Center?"

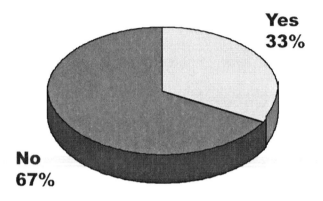

Figure 3: Few interpret the data and do anything with it ... meaning they don't ACT. (Purdue Research Foundation)

Measuring customer satisfaction is a new concept to those companies which have been previously focused almost exclusively on income statements and the balance sheet. Companies now recognize that the new global economy has changed things forever. There is more competition and that competition is fierce. Markets are crowded with products that customers can hardly differentiate. The years of continual sales growth in expanding markets have been replaced by two decades of flattening sales curves. Today's sharp competitors know they have to change their focus. These companies realize that:

- The risk of a customer becoming a "former customer" is extremely high.
- The cost of acquiring a new customer far exceeds the cost of retaining an existing customer.

- Bottom line …the game has changed, and long-standing, satisfied customers are the goal.

Competitors who are going to prosper in this new economic climate increasingly recognize that gathering and analyzing customer satisfaction data is the first step to their prosperity. Only by pinpointing customers' needs, expectations and desires, can they begin to hold on to the customers they have and, as importantly, understand how to better attract new customers. The competitors who will be successful recognize that building the type of customer satisfaction that leads to customer loyalty is a critical strategic weapon that can bring them increased market share and increased profits. They also understand that focusing on customer satisfaction requires a commitment from top management, changes in corporate organization and new values in the corporate culture.

The problem they face, however, is exactly how to do all this and to do it well. They need to know how to quantify, measure and track customer satisfaction. Without a clear and accurate sense of what needs to be measured, how to collect and analyze the data, then use the research results as a strategic weapon to drive the business, the firm cannot be effective in this new business climate. Plans constructed using customer satisfaction research results can be designed to target customers and processes most able to extend profits.

Too many companies rely on outdated and unreliable measures of customer satisfaction. They watch sales volume. They listen to sales reps describe the state of mind of their customers. They track and count frequencies of complaints. They watch accounts receivable aging reports recognizing that unhappy customers pay as late as possible, if at all. While these approaches are not completely without value, they are no substitute for a valid, well-designed customer satisfaction surveying program. It is not surprising, therefore, to find that firms which formally and systematically measure customer satisfaction are usually market leaders (Treacy).

It is also no surprise to find, according to Bienstock and Kahn that the factors that separate market leaders from the rest of the industry are designed to hear the voice of the customer and achieve customer satisfaction. In these companies:

Marketing and sales organizations are primarily responsible (with customer input) for designing customer satisfaction surveying programs, questionnaires and focus groups with the following goals and characteristics:

- Top management and marketing divisions champion the programs.

- Corporate evaluations include both the company's customer satisfaction ratings as well as those of their competitors.

- Satisfaction results are made available to all employees.

- Internal and external quality measures are often tied together.

- Customer satisfaction is incorporated into the strategic focus of the company starting with the mission statement.

- Compensation of all stakeholders is tied directly to the customer satisfaction results.

- A concerted effort is made to relate the customer satisfaction measurement results to internal process metrics.

To be successful, companies need a customer satisfaction surveying system that meets the following criteria:

- The system must be relatively easy to design and understand.

- It must be credible enough that employee performance and compensation can be attached to the final results.

- It must be inexpensive to implement and monitor.

- It must generate actionable reports for management.

The important issue is to think from the 10,000 foot level and realize that as a company, you have many relationships to manage and measure. For instance, study the figure that follows:

Figure 4: Customer Relationship Management. (Purdue Research Foundation)

There are obviously many very important relationships, and continuous improvement must include value analysis, recovery methods, and, of course benchmarking.

It is our goal in this book to provide you with the information you need to institute just such a program in your own company, one that can be used to expand your company's existing sales and marketing information to include the voice of the customer. Interpreting raw customer feedback is an essential step in going from "asking" the customer how you're doing, to "acting" on the resulting feedback. The key then is to

ACT... INTERPRET... and TAKE ACTION!

The Customer Feedback Experience

The customer feedback experience is best first seen in a flowchart as depicted below:

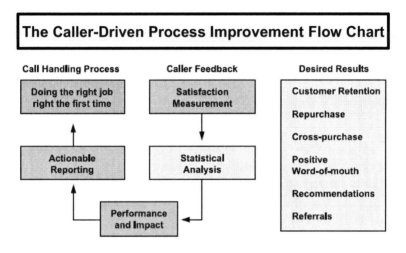

Figure 5: The caller-driven process improvement flowchart. (Purdue Research Foundation)

As we can see from this flowchart, the call handling experience benefits greatly if there is a systematic way to "ask" the caller for their feedback from the call. By having the right statistical analytics in place it becomes possible to interpret this feedback, and immediately turn feedback into actionable reports that will help the contact center be more likely to "do the right thing right the first time"…truly a continuous improvement "flywheel." Also important from this flowchart is the list of desired results, namely:

- **Customer Retention** through increased loyalty;
- Customer **Re-Purchase** of the same product or service;
- Customer **Cross-Purchase** and/or up-sell;
- Positive "**Word of Mouth**" almost making the customer into a company's best sales person;
- Customers make **Recommendations** for your product to others;
- And finally, positive customer **Referrals**.

Literally, results to "die for." Loyal customers, generate more loyal customers, generate more loyal customers …on and on and on.

Turning Customer Feedback into Action

Let's first try to understand why customers leave a company. From studies at Purdue University in the Center for Customer-Driven quality, it has been found over and over again, that most customers disengage from one company and buy the competitor's product due to poor customer service, as show in the next figure:

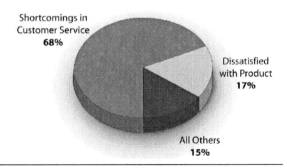

Why do customers leave companies?

Shortcomings in Customer Service
68%

Dissatisfied with Product
17%

All Others
15%

Figure 6: Why do customers leave companies? *(Purdue Research Foundation)*

Notice dissatisfaction with the product is only 17% as compared with over 60% due to one or more poor customer service experiences. By the way, many callers experience poor customer service and thereafter, switch venders. Literally, most customers would rather "switch than fight."

So to better understand why customers leave due to a poor call experience, it is necessary to understand the processes that affect the customer, as shown in the next figure:

Processes that Affect the Customer

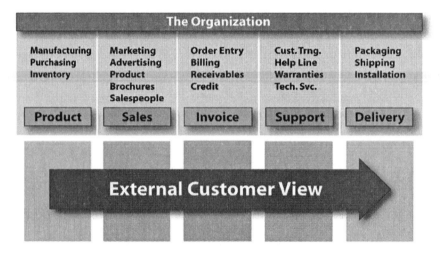

Figure 7: Processes that affect the customer (Purdue Research Foundation)

The classic processes that fit almost every company are:

- using the product;
- buying the product;
- paying for the product;
- getting support for the product;
- and finally, the delivery of the product.

The fact is that the customer service contact center bridges all of these processes because when a customer has a problem with any one of these processes, they of course, call the toll-free number for help.

CHAPTER 2: CUSTOMER FEEDBACK AS A COMPETITIVE DIFFERENTIATOR

Establishing and Maintaining a Difference

Are you ever frustrated or hesitant when you talk to prospective customers because you can't readily explain why they should come to you rather than go to your competitors? Sure, you might have your 30-second elevator speech, but then they ask you that dreaded question, "So what makes you different?" Then, all those self-doubts creep in, and you just aren't sure what to say.

Differentiation can boost confidence--yours in yourself and that prospective customer's confidence in you. Webster's defines differentiate as:

> **Dif-fer-en-ti-ate v. tr. To perceive or show the difference in or between; discriminate.**

In business terms, to differentiate means to create a benefit that customers perceive as being of greater value to them than what they can get elsewhere. It's not enough for you to be different--a potential customer has to take note of the difference and must feel that the difference somehow fits their need better. (Other words that mean virtually the same thing: Competitive Advantage; Unique Selling Proposition; or Value Proposition.)

Sometimes it takes only simple things as shown in Figure 8 on the next page.

Figure 8: Letting customers know that you listen. (Purdue Research Foundation)

As we can see from this figure, the large sign hanging from the ceiling basically says: "hey customers, you told us to allow a check out line without candy, well here it is." Suddenly, customers start thinking this store is different...they listen to us and make changes that we need.

As you develop your business, you can use differentiation to attract more customers. Make a point to evaluate and adjust your differentiation methods at least annually.

The various methods of differentiating your businesses fall into four general categories:

- Price Differentiation;
- Focus Differentiation;
- Product/Service Differentiation; and
- Customer Service Differentiation.

Price Differentiation

Differentiating on price is probably the most common and easily understood method. On the one hand, potential customers might expect a lower price from you than from your larger competition because they perceive you as having less overhead, etc. On the other hand, cheaper prices can evoke perceptions of lower quality, a less-stable business, etc. And if you compete on price against competitors with deeper pockets, you can price yourself right into bankruptcy. Be creative with this differentiator by competing on something other than straight price. For example, you might offer:

- More value--offer more products or services for the same price.
- Freebies --accessories, companion products, free upgrades, and coupons for future purchases.
- Free shipping, etc.--convenience sells, especially when it is free!
- Discounts--includes offering regular sales, coupons, etc. *(see cautions above)*

Focus Differentiation

This is the most important method of differentiation, and in many ways, the easiest. Why? Because you simply can't be everything to everybody, so you must pick a specific way to focus your business. Once you have done that, you can build close relationships with key customers that will be hard to duplicate. For example, you might differentiate yourself through:

- Location--take advantage your closeness to prospective customers.
- Customer specialization--be very specific about what characteristics your customers will have-for

example, racing bicycle enthusiasts or companies with a spiritual conscience.

- Customer relationships--know customers really well, form partnerships with them, and get them to speak for you!
- Affinity relationships--associate your product/service with a well-known person or organization.
- One-stop shopping--offer everything your target market needs, in your area of expertise.
- Wide selection (within your niche)-although this one may seem to be the opposite of focus--the key is to be very specific in one dimension and very broad in another.

Product/Service Offering Differentiation

How much you are able to differentiate your product or service offering will vary based on what type of business you are in. For instance, if you are in a highly regulated business, your options may be limited. Explore a totally new market or type of product or service, however, and the possibilities abound.

The key to successful differentiation in this category, again, is to know your customers, really, really well. Talk to them often, and you will know what they need most and be able to offer it, long before your competitors know what is happening. For example, your product or service could stand out in one of these ways:

Quality--create a product or service that is exceptional in one or more ways. Examples:

- Lasts longer;
- Better;
- Easier to use;

- Safer;
- New/First--be the first one to offer something in your location/field;
- Features/Options--offer lots of choices, unusual combinations, or solve a problem for a customer in a way no one else does;
- Customization-- you may be able to more easily handle special orders than your competitors.

Customer Feedback as the Competitive Edge

Build your reputation on making customers feel really good about doing business with you.

Examples:

- Deliver Fast--next day, or one-hour--make it faster than customers think possible.
- Unique channel—offer and support your products & services using multiple touch-points ... i.e., email, internet Web site, internet chat, fax-back, kiosk ...not just over the phone.
- Service-delight customers!--it may seem expensive to offer exceptional service--but it pays off in word-of-mouth advertising.
- Before/during/after-sales support--provide technical or other support to customers using your product. -- You might contract with a third-party to provide that support--but customers will perceive it as being from you!
- Guarantee/warranty--offer 100% money-back, or free replacement parts.
- YOU--offer yourself & your management team, together with your collective blend of unique talents and skills, to attract customers. Make sure they can get access to you, too!

Keys to Successful Differentiation:

- Know your customers, really, really well.
- Pick a blend of differentiation methods that, in the eyes of your customers, truly sets you apart.
- Talk about your differentiation in terms of customer benefits.
- Tell everyone about what differentiates you--often.
- Keep your differentiation fresh by listening for changing customer needs.*(20)*

Customers seek equity with product and service providers. If they feel that they've paid a price that equals the quality they've received, all is right with the marketplace. However, if the quality of their purchase is at an extreme -- less than or greater than they expected it to be -- customers feel motivated to regain balance in the buyer-seller equation.

Companies allocate significant resources to customer satisfaction measurement and improvement.

Wayne Hoyer, chairman of the marketing department at University of Texas-Austin's McCombs School of Business, says satisfaction with product or service quality has a strong and positive impact on customers' willingness to pay. In fact, the longer customers have been satisfied with a brand or its maker, the more they'll pay, his research has shown:

"It is increasingly more difficult in today's environment to get any kind of differentiation," Hoyer says. *"If anything can achieve it, however, branding combined with a unique customer service bundle can!"*

Chapter 3: Understanding the Target Customer

No matter what technologies you try to use to help provide good customer service, and no matter what training you provide, or other steps you may take, you don't stand a chance of improving customer service if you don't understand your customers, and customers in general. The reality is there are a lot of misconceptions about what customers want, and what constitutes good customer service. In this chapter, you'll find questions and answers to help you understand customer needs, wants, and perceptions.

Customer Psychology

If you want customers to perceive that you are giving them good customer service, or excellent customer service, you need to understand them, and look at what you offer from their point of view. So, what do customers want?

Customers want:

- Problem solved;
- Effort;
- Acknowledgement and understanding;
- Choices and options;
- Positive surprises;
- Consistency, reliability, and predictability;
- Value (not necessarily best price);
- Reasonable simplicity;
- Speed;
- Confidentiality; and
- Sense of importance.

Discovering the Customers' Psychology

Product placement! Lifestyle marketing! Integrated promotions! It seems that everywhere you look these days some marketer is trying to get you to buy a product by appealing to your psyche rather than explicitly advertising it. As technology continues to pervade our daily lives, the lines between sales, marketing, advertising and entertainment are rapidly blurring. The big payback for marketers is to get into your head and influence your behavior by augmenting traditional marketing and advertising with an appeal to your psyche.

Customer Segmentation: The Key to Customer Psychology

Here's the rub: all customers are not created equal and as such it's not so easy to understand what actually drives purchasing behavior. Indeed Business Week recently ran a cover story on the psychology of the male consumer (Business Week, 09/04/06, Revealed! Secrets of the Male Shopper). But certainly not all consumers are men. And not all consumers purchase all products. And even if you have a handle on who purchases your product, not all customers are equally valuable (profitable + strategically important). As such, the key to effecting behavior via customer psychology is rock solid customer segmentation.

Customer segmentation is the key to making the customer the CRM design point, leveraging CRM effectiveness (doing better things), as opposed to simply implementing operational technology (e.g., sales automation) that largely addresses efficiency (doing things quicker).

At its most basic level, segmentation involves classifying customers with similar characteristics into groups (called "segments") and then dealing with the segments instead of individual customers (especially important in organizations with large customer bases, where individual customer scrutiny would be virtually impossible).

The key reason for segmentation is the development of informed, segment-specific customer lifecycle treatments as well as a better understanding of which industries and markets should be served and which should be lowest priority going forward.

Most importantly, segmentation guides future interaction with customers, based on the organization's deeper understanding of each segment's customer's profitability, behavior, industry context, and lifetime value. Companies also use segmentation to prioritize new product development efforts, develop customized marketing programs, choose specific product features, establish appropriate service options, design an optimal distribution strategy, and determine appropriate product pricing.

Customer segmentation begins with the identification and collection of pertinent data elements (classification variables) and assumes that IT and marketing professionals will work closely together in data gathering strategies:

Segmenting based on customer value:

Revenue generated from the customer's transactions, cost to acquire and retain the customer, customer's credit worthiness, resulting profit from the customer, and the customer's need for interactions (cost to serve).

Segmenting based on demographic issues:

Describing customers in terms of their personal characteristics, such as age, gender, income, ethnicity, marital status, education, and occupation.

Segmenting based on geographical issues:

Describing customers in terms of their physical location, such as city, state, ZIP code, U.S. Census tract, county, region, and metropolitan/suburban/rural location

Segmentation based on psychographic issues:

Describing customers in terms of personality traits, such as attitudes, lifestyle, aversion to risk, and TV programs watched.

Segmentation based on behavioral issues:

Emphasizes what customers have purchased and can suggest what other products they may be interested in; this includes brand loyalty, usage level, benefits sought, and distribution channels used.

Segmentation data emphasizes what customers have purchased and can suggest what other products they may be interested in; this includes brand loyalty, usage level, benefits sought, and distribution channels used.

Furthermore, this data is then used to generate customer segments, with additional qualification based on the current and future financial contribution each customer represents to the company. Further refinement of these initial customer segments must be planned.

When customer segments have been developed, a CRM treatment (customer pattern) can then be developed to ultimately create exit barriers and gain channel efficiencies along the way.

However, there is a "chicken or the egg" information conundrum because most organizations do not have enough information to profile their customers, therefore, designing around the customer requires information to create customer patterns.

This can be a vicious circle and avoiding this conundrum means that even without perfect information, organizations must start somewhere and use that as an opportunity to collect information along the way, updating the segment/ treatments iteratively.

What Is the Right Number of Segments to Have?

There is no definitive answer to this question. Experience, intuition, statistical results, and common sense all must be applied to decide on the number of segments to retain. If there are numerous very small segments, the segmentation criteria may need adjustment.

Too many segments can lead to the development of too many different (i.e., expensive) marketing programs for small, very similar markets. However, several rules of thumb can be used to determine the appropriate number of segments. Segments must be:

- **Large enough:** The majority of segments must be large enough to be economically support marketing and product design efforts.

- **Relevant**: The segments must be relevant to the company's products/services.

- **Reachable**: Segments must be reachable through one or more mixes of marketing variables (price, promotion, features, and distribution).

- **Differentiable:** Clearly defined differences among customer segments must exist to make some segments more desirable than others.

Although determining a segmentation strategy is very much a business issue, technologies can be brought to bear to make this task somewhat easier:

- . Data mining and behavior modeling using predictive analysis technologies built into campaign management tools can help marketers move from declarative segmentation (segmenting based on database fields) to predictive segmentation (segmenting based on mathematical algorithms), enabling more "creative" segmentation.

- . Optimization technologies providing nonlinear, constraint-based optimization to enable mathematical calculation of best customer/segment, best offer, and best campaign.

As we have seen, organizations must understand customer psychology to truly make the customer the CRM design point. This notion is enabled by creating value-based customer segments and applying appropriately "sized" CRM life-cycle treatments. (21)

Customer Surveying: The Foundation Concepts

There are some basic concepts in customer surveying that should be reviewed. These are related to fundamentals of surveying and statistical principles. Not much can be accomplished without them. In fact, if we don't focus on fundamentals, we may end up embarrassed like the manager shown in the next figure.

"I think you should be more explicit about what happened in February."

Figure 9: Your analytics should help explain change. (Purdue Research Foundation)

Foundation Statistical Concepts

Before we get to the actual analysis procedures, and there are a number of options, it is important that you are acquainted with several important statistical concepts that will aid you in making good decisions.

The goal of a well-designed customer satisfaction surveying program is to learn what to improve or reengineer in order to change your products and services so that customer satisfaction will be increased, thus increasing customer retention. To generalize from a particular study to the complete population of customers, appropriate sampling techniques must be implemented. Although there are other types of samples than random samples (stratified, cluster, area probability, etc.), we will focus on random samples in the following section because with a sample that is truly random, sampling error can be calculated and confidence limits can be placed on estimates of satisfaction. Without such a sample, the statistical techniques used by most software programs are not applicable. Also, if the sample is representative, inferences based on the sample results can be validly applied to the population and that is the reason for using samples instead of surveying the entire customer base in the first place.

The concept is simple and best described by the next figure.

Every moment-of-truth counts

Customer Service	Customer Perception	Satisfaction Level
Contacting a Company's Call Center	Better than Expected →	Delighted
	As Expected →	Satisfied
	Less than Expected →	Dissatisfied

Figure 10: Every moment of truth counts. (Purdue Research Foundation)

In this figure, it is clear that for every call experience, the caller has certain expectations, and the agent either meets these expectation, exceeds these expectation, and or lastly could fails to be anywhere close to the caller's expectation. This immediately and logically give rise to the caller being either delighted, satisfied, or dissatisfied.

Defining the Sample

In this section we will differentiate between the concepts of "initial sample" and "final sample." The initial sample is the list of those customers you plan to, and eventually do, contact for the study. The final sample consists only of those customers who were both contacted and were willing to respond.

Relationship between Population, Initial Sample, and Final Sample

Figure 11 demonstrates the relationship between the population of all your customers, the initial sample and the final sample. As you can see, the initial sample is a subset of all your customers, and the final sample is, in turn, a subset of the initial sample (unless, of course, you attain a 100% response rate to the survey).

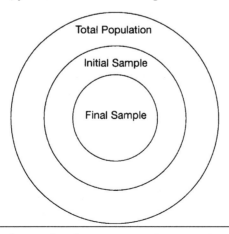

Figure 11: Relationship between population, initial sample, and final sample. (Purdue Research Foundation)

The question of sample size can be better appreciated in Figure 12.

How many spectators would you have to survey?

Figure 12: How many of the audience would you have to survey?
(Purdue Research Foundation)

If you wanted to survey this audience regarding the seat that they purchased, how many of these spectators would have to be interview? Since conducting survey is not inexpensive, the goal is to interview as few as possible.

Constructing Random Samples

The first determinant of survey quality is whether or not you are contacting a truly random sample of customers. If you are, you can use various statistical techniques to describe and predict the behavior of customers and estimate the amount of error in your data (just as television or newspaper surveys are reported with a margin of error, e.g., +/- 3%).

The ability of random samples to allow calculations of sampling error depends on large samples being drawn for the study. Random drawing of small samples does not provide the same benefit. Simply put, the idea is that if you draw at random enough times, eventually you will draw a sample that is representative or reflective of the population from which the sample is drawn.

For example, if you are the U.S. government and you draw a random sample of tax payers to ascertain their views on tax reform, you could go to the rolls of the IRS and, using a computer program, randomly draw 5,000 taxpayer names and addresses. In all likelihood, with a sample this large, the views of all U.S. taxpayers will be represented in roughly the same proportions as exist in the population as a whole.

The key consideration here is that all taxpayers have a known (non-zero) chance of being included in the study (preferably an equal chance). A random sample also implies that selection is not related to interviewer discretion or taxpayer characteristics such as availability or attitude. We made sure of this in our example by having the computer draw the sample.

The main issue initially is to decide on two items, namely: what do you want your confidence level to be, and how accurate does the final conclusion have to be. A very typical setting for business decision is to focus on a 95% level of confidence, with an error rate of +/- 5%. The table that follows is algorithmically derived and you can see the number wanted is a random selected sample size determination is 384 participants completing the survey.

Margin of Error

Confidence	10%	5%	3%	2%	1%
80%	41	164	455	1024	4096
90%	68	272	756	1702	6806
95%	96	384	1067	2401	9604
98%	136	548	1508	3393	13572
99%	166	666	1849	4160	16641

Table 1: Determining sample size (Purdue Research Foundation)

A 95% level of confidence in the resulting data means, quite simply, that a manager making a decision based on this statistically-derived answer will be correct 19 times out of 20 situation ... not a bad average for any executive constructing an initial sample that is random means using probability methods to select customers for inclusion in a study. Three possible scenarios are:

1. From an existing list of customers, picking every nth name or having a computer randomly pick customers from a database.

2. Using a table of random numbers to select from your client list, i.e., simply list your customers in order from first (1) to last (n). Then, pick a number from the table and match it to the customer's number on the list.

3. Interviewing every nth customer or client about his or her experiences.

We know of a school district that samples by family rather than by student when gathering information from parents. This is done because many families have more than one student in a school, and the more students from a family, the greater that family's chance of selection for the study, thus introducing bias based on the number of students in a family.

In designing a random sample, it all comes down to this one essential question:

> *"Am I constructing my initial sample from my customer list so that everyone on the list has an equal (or known) chance of inclusion?"*

The actual physical act of selecting a random initial sample will depend upon whether you are using a database on a computer or not. If you are, then you can use statistical programs like Statistical Package for the Social Sciences (SPSS), Statistical Application Software (SAS) and others to generate a random sample from a customer list. If you are not, then you can use a systematic random sample (every nth name) to physically construct the sample listing.

Regardless of you draw your sample, the most important "end goal" is to make sure you end up with 384 completed surveys. As shown in the figure below, to end with 384 completed surveys, you may have to begin with a much larger sample number.

**Relationship between Population, Initial
Sample, and Final Sample**

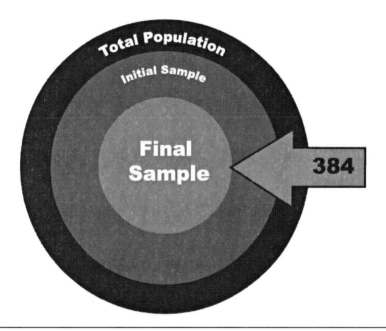

*Figure 13: Relationship between population, initial sample size,
and final sample size. (Purdue Research Foundation)*

Response rate vary based on the method of survey fielding
(more later), but often to actually end up with 384 surveys, you
may have to begin with 1,000 persons who you will approach to
complete the survey.

Attaining Representative Samples

The second determinant of the quality of a data-gathering
program is whether or not it allows you to contact a representative
sample of your customers.

For ease of illustration, let us imagine that you area computer
mail-order house and that the customer base is segmented into
three groups: household users, business users and government/not-
for-profit users. In such a case, you will likely want both the initial

31

sample and the final sample to be drawn from those three segments in proportion to their size since it is likely that each of these three groups has very different customer needs. When this is accomplished, you can say that your sample is representative (at least with respect to the limited set of criteria used to segment the customers).

How a representative sample is attained will vary from organization to organization. The concept of representativeness simply means that along the pre-defined characteristics, your sample mirrors the characteristics of the population to which you wish to generalize your research results. Here are some examples to further clarify these issues.

Many hotels place cards in guest rooms to gather information on guests' satisfaction with the room, meal, and services. Note here that the initial sample and the population are the same. Who is likely to complete such questionnaires? Research clearly shows the customers who are the most likely to respond are those who are very satisfied or dissatisfied (that is, at the extremes). Those who do not hold strong opinions are unlikely to bother to answer so we will learn very little about their experiences. What this shows is that the hotel's final sample of customers is biased and not representative of all types of customers. Placing a card in each room did not make the sample representative because not every customer even notices the card unless there is a reason to, i.e., the customer is very satisfied or dissatisfied.

Using an existing database of customers, a bank decides to call customers by phone. If someone is not reached after two calls, the bank drops the customer's name from the study and substitutes someone else. In this instance, a bias is created against the inclusion of people who either (a) are not home at the times when interviewers call, such as two-earner households, (b) are generally busy people, or (c) use telephone answering machines to screen their calls. If such customers are different in their attitudes toward the bank than those more easily contacted, information is being lost and the sample is not representative.

As a third example, let us say a department store mails a questionnaire to all of their charge card customers. That plan is fine, but not all customers have the store's charge card. Therefore, those not holding the charge card have no chance of being contacted for the study, so the survey cannot be representative of all customers. In this instance, again, the population (all charge card holders) and the initial sample are the same. Additionally, the final sample is likely to be representative (i.e., reflective) of the population from which it was drawn; that is, representative of customers who hold their charge card, but not representative of all customers.

Note that it is quite possible to have a non-representative sample but to still draw that sample at random. If the department store management wished to generalize the results of the study to all customers, then drawing the sample by whatever means from the list of credit card holders could not result in a representative sample. Drawing every nth name from the credit card list would lead to an unbiased sample of credit card holders, but could not lead to a sample that is representative of all customers. Therefore whether representativeness has been achieved is a function of the population from which the sample was drawn and the population to which results are to be generalized and not a function of the actual routine used to draw the sample.

Creating a sample that is completely representative of the population of your customers is not always possible. This is not necessarily a problem so long as you understand a sample's limitations. This is technically called the sampling frame: it is the list of the population elements from which the sample will be drawn. While the sampling frame is often self-evident, it is important not to take it for granted. Take, for example, a dog food manufacturer that conducted a large marketing study to determine what was wanted in a dog food, including packaging characteristics. A major campaign was launched and sales poured in. But a month later sales fell dramatically. In a later test conducted by a professional firm, it was found that dogs hated the taste of the food. The real customers were never consulted!

In summary, you must always ask yourself these two questions about your survey methodology:

- "Does it include all types of customers?"

- "If not, who am I leaving out?"

CHAPTER 4: CUSTOMER FEEDBACK EXCELLENCE

Critical Success Factors

The critical success factors of a customer satisfaction measurement and management process are shown in the next figure.

Figure 14: Critical Success Factors. (Purdue Research Foundation)

This figure emphasizes the complexity of a comprehensive customer satisfaction process, and the need for each of these "pieces" to be in place. Of course, the end result of a working customer feedback system is a contact center that provides quality services and enhances customer re-purchase as shown in the next figure.

Customer Situation	Re-Purchase Probability
Product with no problems	78%
Product with problems and an ineffective Customer Care Center (calls and e -mails)	32%
Product with problems and an effective Customer Care Center	89%

©BenchmarkPortal Inc./Purdue University

Figure 15: The rewards of an effective customer care center

In Figure 15 we see that a product supported by an effective customer care center imbues greater customer re-purchase intentions than a so-called perfect product. To fully realize the value of this achievement let's view the next figure which is the result of research conducted at Harvard University.

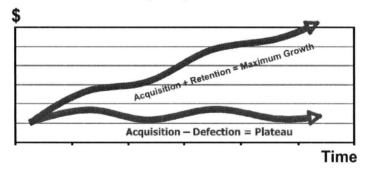

Customer Loyalty Impacts Profit

Acquisition + Retention = Maximum Growth

Acquisition — Defection = Plateau

Source: Harvard Business Review

Figure 16: Customer loyalty improves profits. (Purdue Research Foundation)

36

Most top executives are the first to admit that they expect as much as 80% of next years revenue must comes from this year's customers, yet they often will not spend the money to build and operate an effective customer service contact center. Yet in the kind of research shown in Figure 16, it is clear that customer retention plus customer acquisition maximize growth and profits. Similar studies conduct by market researchers at IBM have shown that a 5% increase in customer retention can increase profits by as much as 100%.

Defining Customer Touchpoints

A customer touchpoint is defined as any experience when the customer reaches out and "touches" the company, or the company reaches out and "touches" the customer. Both uses of the word "touch" are, of course, figurative. These customer touchpoints fall into definable categories, as follows:

Face-to-Face

The face-to-face touchpoint typically occurs at a retail store, a branch office, or even when the company's employee delivers a product or service directly to the customer's office or home. The key element is that the customer and a representative of the company are talking face-to-face, and in person.

Telephone

This is the most popular touchpoint between customers and companies for most companies. With the onset of toll-free numbers to call, and the ubiquitous access to the telephone, customers freely call companies before, during, and after the purchase of a product. The advent of the wireless cell phone has more than doubled this access channel, or touchpoint.

Email

Email is the fastest growing touchpoint channel now that the world's population is becoming totally Internet-enabled. Though a popular touchpoint, research shows that email is the least efficient touchpoint channel due to the fact that most consumers can not read and/or write very well.

Chat

Chat is an interesting new touchpoint channel. Once a customer is already on a company's Website, the natural goal is to keep them there. Chat allows a natural interaction between the Website visitor and the live agent on an as-needed basis.

Web Self-Service

An obvious goal for most companies today is to encourage customers to "help themselves" wherever and how ever possible. The company's Website is a perfect touchpoint channel through which customers can find answers to questions, explore product information, and place product orders.

Kiosk

Finally coming of age is the customer service kiosk touchpoint channel. The beauty of the kiosk is that it is a "window into the company" that can be place at strategic locations, preferably selected based on the likelihood that a customer would need to interact with a company at that point. Examples might be: hotel and airport lobbies, retail store isles, shopping malls, and train stations.

Distributor, Dealer, Retailer

Many companies distribute their product through the chain of distributors, dealers, and finally retailers. Each of these is a potential customer touchpoint that whose quality of service needs to be measured and managed.

CHAPTER 5: MANAGING CUSTOMER RELATIONSHIPS

Measuring the Customer Experience through Feedback

Every day, companies fall short when it comes to understanding their customers, competitors and markets. They rely on intuition to guess their customers' needs and experiences. They attempt to piece together disparate information sources to understand their competitors. They make strategic decisions based on unreliable ten-person focus groups or — worse—in a vacuum. That's a shame. Without a clear picture of their customers, their competitors and their markets, companies make bad business decisions, get blindsided by the competition, and lose profitable customers.

In an annual survey of thousands of contact centers, BenchmarkPortal asked contact center managers the following questions. You may or may not find their aggregated responses surprising:

Question 1: "Does your contact center have a formal process to collect the caller's satisfaction regarding their experience with how their call was handled?

Their responses are depicted in the following chart:

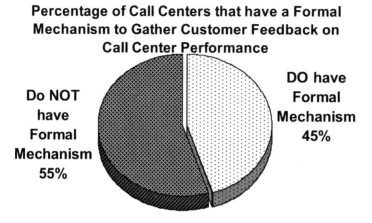

Percentage of Call Centers that have a Formal Mechanism to Gather Customer Feedback on Call Center Performance

Figure 17. Contact centers that have a formal mechanism to gather customer feedback. (Purdue Research Foundation)

Finding: Nine out-of-every twenty contact centers across All Industries **do not** have a formal mechanism for gathering customer feedback on contact center performance to determine the level of customer satisfaction.

Interpretation: Internal key performance indicators can only tell management part of the story of how well they are serving their customers. In today's competitive world, customer satisfaction is a more significant market differentiator and competitive advantage than product features or price. No company can attain best practices certification without the presence of a formal customer satisfaction mechanism to collect customer feedback in place.

BenchmarkPortal next asked those who answered "Yes" the following two questions:

Question 2: "Within the past 90 days, what percentage of your callers gave you a perfect score for customer satisfaction (e.g., a perfect score of 5 out of 5, or a perfect score of 7 out of 7)?

(Note: The Best of All Industries Average represents those contact centers that are in the upper quartile (25%) of their industry sector as compared to their peers.)

Callers that gave a Perfect Score for Customer Satisfaction within the Past 90 Days

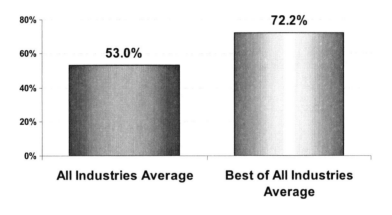

Figure 18. Percent perfect customer satisfaction perfect scores.
(Purdue Research Foundation)

Finding:	The Best of All Industries Average is 37% better than the All Industries Average in perfect customer satisfaction scores given within the past 90 days.
Interpretation:	The best metric to be used for measuring the "true" level of customer satisfaction is the percentage of customers/callers who give a perfect score, provided that a valid statistical sample is taken.

Question 3: "Within the past 90 days, what percentage of your callers gave you the lowest score for customer satisfaction *(e.g., a low score of 1 out of 5, or a low score of 1 out of 7)?*

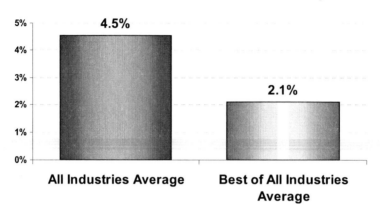

Callers that gave a Perfect Score for Customer Satisfaction within the Past 90 Days

Figure 19. Percent callers that gave the lowest score for customer satisfaction. (Purdue Research Foundation)

Finding: The percentage of low customer satisfaction scores for the Best of All Industries is 54% lower than that of All Industries.

Interpretation: Tracking lowest scores is the flip side of collecting perfect customer satisfaction scores, and essential to the quality monitoring process of a contact center. The next step is to classify these contacts by category/agent, and feed the results into the agent coaching and training process to remedy the root causes.

42

This survey clearly indicated that a large percentage of contact centers do not have a true picture of how the contact experience is perceived by their customers.

How then, one must ask, do these companies expect to maintain a competitive position with their rivals? Also, how much lost revenue are they experiencing as their customer base shrinks, abandoning them for competitors who want their business and reflect that desire in the manner that they treat their customers?

The primary mission of customer service is to engineer each call in such a way as to delight the caller. Delight results in an increasing probability of customer retention, hence increasing the customer lifetime value and willingness to recommend your product or service to others.

Your customers experience a 'Moment Of Truth' (MOT) every time they call your contact center for assistance. In Figure 10, we diagrammed the measurement of the telephonic MOT by determining internal and external metrics, which can be used as online feedback to those specific process managers that support the contact center and impact this critical MOT for your callers.

An MOT is any and every event where a customer might experience and access the performance of your product or service. An MOT is both a data gathering and a decision-generating event. The customer metaphorically stands at the crossroads and decides to reuse or recommend your contact center to others or vows to never use the contact center service again.

Of course, the real threat is not a decision never to use the contact center again, but rather a decision to discontinue use of the core service/product of the company. Such a decision would lead inevitably to replacement by a competitor's offering..

The findings from our research suggest that measuring the caller's perception of the call is best done immediately after the call has been completed rather than hours, days, or weeks later. In this way, it is most possible to capture the caller's actual experience at the MOT.

We have found that a comprehensive, well-designed, and well-executed customer satisfaction (a.k.a., customer satisfaction or CS) measurement program can generate reliable external metrics which can be driven into internal business process metrics as shown in Figure 20.

Connecting Caller Perception to Internal Call Center Metrics

Caller Perceptible Metrics	Caller Expectations	Call Center Processes	Internal Metrics
ASA Hold Time Transfers Queue Time More	5 rings No transfers No Hold Time Short queue	Recruiting Hiring Training Routing	IAHT ACWT C/A/H Turnover More ... ...

Figure 20: Relationship of Caller Perception to Call Center Metrics. (Purdue Research Foundation)

A CS measurement program can also ensure that quality improvement initiatives are properly focused on issues that are most important to the caller. The direct objective of a CS measurement program is to generate valid and consistent caller feedback; i.e., to quantify the perception of the caller which can then be used to initiate positive service strategies.

In trying to better understand what is going to be measured and how the results relate to loyalty and repurchase, we have found it important to approximate the mind-set of customers. Recall from Figure 5 that in general, the customer's mind-set will fall in one of three measurable categories:

- Rejection—Very likely to take business elsewhere.
- Acceptance—Service is adequate, but given another alternative customer will probably leave.
- Preference—These are the loyal customers you must strive to retain! When given a choice, you will be selected more often.

An important theme of the external metrics CS measurement is to identify attributes for improvement that will increase your ability to move customers from the acceptance category to the preference category. As we will see later, customers who prefer you are actually a quantifiable asset to the company.

Seeing the CS measurement program as an integral part of continuous quality improvement is crucial to demonstrating the return on investment (ROI) of the contact center as follows:

1. Through selecting the process or processes for change that will maximize the impact on customer satisfaction and loyalty;
2. By preventing erosion of the customer base;
3. By increasing the occurrence of recommendations;
4. By minimizing negative word-of-mouth; and
5. By better understanding what the customer perceives to be value-added.

We need to clearly contrast the internal metrics from the external metrics. Internal metrics are generated by computers internal to your PBX, ACD, or VRU or through departments such as Human Resources and Accounting. They are "hard" numbers that deal with precise reality. For instance, the average queue time today was 6 minutes and 42 seconds. There were .6 transfers per call. The abandon rate was 3%. Agent turnover was 22% last year. The average cost per call last year was $5.67.

External metrics do not have the exactness that can be attributed to a computer or an accounting system, but instead are the "soft" numbers of caller perception that express opinions or emotions which means qualitative measures. Average queue time may have been 6 minutes and 42 seconds, but the customer may perceive it as 15 minutes and way too long. This is the reality the customer will use in decision making for repurchase, recommendation, and continued loyalty. Therefore, we should apply the axiom, "It's not nearly as important what is true, as what the caller thinks is true."

However, we do not wish to give the impression that caller perception cannot be measured to an accuracy sufficient to make difficult decisions. Quite the contrary is true. In a properly designed customer satisfaction survey, we can ascertain the mindset of a population of callers to within an accuracy of 95% allowing managers to make reasonable, consistent decisions from a caller CS program. Accuracy to a 95% level essentially means that conclusions made using this qualitative caller data will be correct 19 times out of 20 tries. Not bad for most decision makers!

A Model of the CS Process

There are four factors that determine satisfaction with various service attributes, and these in turn influence overall satisfaction, willingness to recommend, and repurchase intention (the three principal global CS measures). The factors are;

- service quality,

- expectations, attribute importance,

- past experience (problems/no problems with the service/product), and

- various demographic variables like type of customer, length of relationship with your products, gender, income, and age. See Figure 14 for a diagram of our model of the CS process.

Note these critical features about our model:

1. Service expectations are driven by the segment variables, such as business-to-business versus business-to-consumer accounts, as well as by previous satisfaction experiences. For example, customers with large monthly accounts may expect a different level of service from the contact center than those with much smaller accounts. Expectations for service are generally formed by past experiences with other contact centers including, but not limited to, your contact center. Expectations are also impacted by word-of-mouth and competitive offerings.

2. Service attributes (or characteristics) have no significant effect on customer expectations. Rather the customers' evaluations of the service attributes combine to create performance ratings. The performance ratings are inputs, which drive the overall satisfaction rating. The effect of the attributes on overall satisfaction will then be derived using regression analysis.

3. We suggest the demographic variables do not usually affect attribute satisfaction directly, but indirectly through expectations and attribute importance. Again, customers who use your larger, more complex products and services or pay larger fees may place more importance on available contact center customer services than other customers, which in turn will influence their overall satisfaction. Consequently, as the CS program expands in the future, the same type of CS analysis can be repeated on the various segmented customer groups to identify differences.

The obvious goal of the CS surveying program is to define, refine, and ultimately provide quality telephonic service for all callers. This does not necessarily mean providing the same level of service for everyone. A bank does not supply the same services at no cost to those with modest accounts as it does for the big investor, but it should strive to provide segment-specific quality service.

Calculating Performance Scores

We recommend re-coding the customer survey responses into a 100-point scale. When presenting results of performance, it is generally easier for the audience to understand the meaning of a 100-point scale. Figures 21 and 22 are common data transformations.

Original Scale Value	Re-coded Value
1	0.0
2	11.1
3	22.2
4	33.3
5	44.4
6	55.5
7	66.6
8	77.7
9	88.8
10	100.0

Figure 21. Transformation of data from 1–10 to 1–100. (Purdue Research Foundation)

Original Scale Value	Re-coded Value
1	0
2	25
3	50
4	75
5	100

Figure 22. Transformation of data from 1–5 to 1–100. (Purdue Research Foundation)

After re-coding the original scale, the performance is quantified by calculating the mean for each service attribute, overall satisfaction, willingness to continue service, and willingness to recommend.

The performance scores are important, but they are only part of the necessary management information. Of course performance results pinpoint the service attributes on which the agents receive low scores. However, a more effective analysis would be to determine which service attributes are contributing to the three primary drivers of customer retention:

1. Overall satisfaction

2. Willingness to recommend

3. Repurchase intentions

In order to examine each attribute's contribution to the overall picture, a multiple regression analysis must be conducted. Regression analysis allows all attributes to be considered in a single equation which is a much more attractive option than conducting a long series of correlation analyses repetitively examining the relationships between pairs of variables.

In attempting to define callers' overall satisfaction ratings, we can build a model to include all of the service variables. "Overall satisfaction" is a function of the attributes listed in Figure 20. The attributes listed correspond to the surveyed CS items.

In the next figure, let's review once more the concept of customer satisfaction.

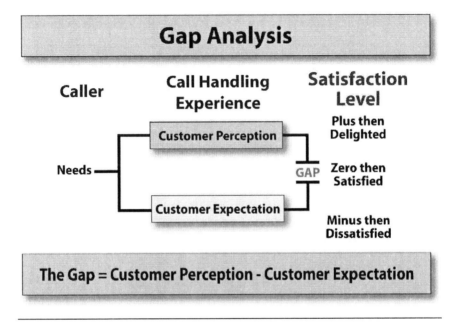

Figure 23: Gap analysis leading to change initiatives. (Purdue Research Foundation)

We begin by "interpreting" the voice of the customer to determine where there are gaps in the performance of the call handling experience.

As can be seen in the next figure, the contact center must strive for "top box" performance, which means analyzing what percent of callers give your agents a 5 out-of 5, meaning a perfect score.

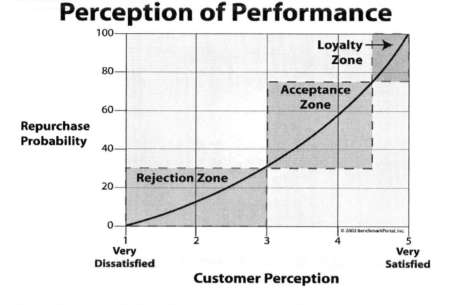

Figure 24: Turning customer perception into quantitative results for analysis. (Purdue Research Foundation)

The fact remains that the real challenge of a customer satisfaction methodology is to determine how to minimize "horrible" experiences, and to maximize "exceptional" experiences in call handling as shown in the next figure.

Distribution of Caller Experiences

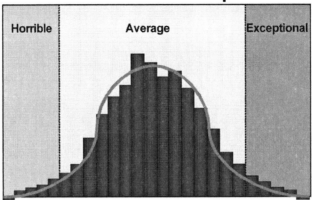

Actual Service Experience
Distribution of Caller Experiences

Figure 25: A normal distribution of caller experiences. (Purdue Research Foundation)

The shape of this "bell curve" will vary in terms of breadth and/or height, but we will always have many of our callers giving us a 2, 3, or 4 out of five, versus a 1 or a 5, meaning the worst and the best scores.

The analysis is specifically focused on determining which attributes are affecting overall satisfaction ratings at a statistically significant level.

The next figure depicts the relationship between averages, means, medians, and impact, a key point to understand as we move forward with the interpretation process.

Understanding the Impact Factor

The lowest mean score on a survey may NOT always be what is most important for your company.

Variables

Impact

Statistics

"The squeaky wheel gets the grease"

Figure 26: Understanding the "impact" factor. (Purdue Research Foundation)

Those attributes in Figures 25 and 26, which are statistically affecting satisfaction with the service interaction, are marked by the asterisk (*). These are significant at the 95% confidence level. If that attribute also has a performance score of less than 85, a need for improvement has been identified.

Customer Service Attributes: CSR

	Impact	Performance
Quickly Understood*	.25	70
Showed Concern*	.20	60
Spoke Clearly	.10	80
Product Knowledge	.05	70

1.0   *statistically significant impact on satisfaction   100%

Figure 27: Attribute Performance and Impact—Example 1. (Purdue Research Foundation)

A clear presentation of the regression results is critical. We recommend a two-sided bar chart so that the users of the report can see the performance scores along with each attribute's respective affect on overall satisfaction. Figure 27 presents results pertaining to the agent. This is how the multiple regression results should be interpreted:

1. The chart indicates that two attributes are statistically impacting satisfaction: the agent "quickly understood" the customer's situation and "showed concern" for the customer when answering questions. These two attributes then become the focus for management action. Improvement efforts should not be made on attributes that are not statistically impacting overall satisfaction.

2. Looking at the performance side of the chart, it is apparent that neither significant attribute is achieving the desired level of 85.

3. How are these two attributes subsequently prioritized for action? Their respective impacts on satisfaction are close at .25 versus .20. This suggests they are each important to satisfaction ratings and to nearly the same degree. However, the performance scores for the item "showed concern" is at 60 whereas the item "quickly understood" is at 70, so a manager may wish to focus on first improving the scores for "showed concern." It is always wise for a manager to address the issues that require the least amount of financial investment. Gaining small victories is important for the contact center manager, the teams, and the CS program.

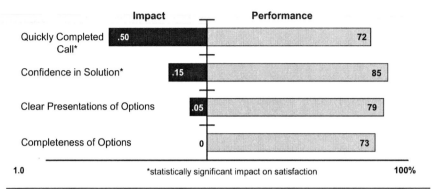

Figure 28. Attribute Performance and Impact—Example 2. (Purdue Research Foundation)

The results presented in Figure 28 would lead the manager to consider upgrading the training for empathy and listening skills. If you have a quality control team that monitors calls, then they may be able to add yet another perspective. Reviewing the customers' comments from the open-ended survey questions may provide further ideas of what specific agent skills could be improved.

How can you use the results and begin to diagnose the cause for the customers' perceptions? We have constructed Figure 29 to suggest some of the general areas of focus when improvement opportunities are identified by the multiple regression and performance scores.

Possible Focus for Improvement if Performance Score is Below 85%	Service Attribute Measured by CS Survey
	Agent:
• listening skills	• quickly understood customer's
• empathy skills	request
• telephone techniques	• showed concern when
• product training	answering questions
• communication techniques	• spoke clearly
• telephone techniques	• product/service knowledge
• telephone, communication	**Answer/Solution Provided:**
techniques, system improvement	• completeness of answer
• system training, system	• customer's confidence in
improvement issue	solution provided
	• clear presentation of options
	• quickly completed call

Figure 29: Suggested action based upon survey results. (Purdue Research Foundation)

Results presented in Figure 29 focus on the service attributes of the answer/solution provided. Similar to the above discussion, first focus on the attributes that are statistically impacting satisfaction; i.e., those that reflect caller delight and ultimately, retention. The number of attributes that are statistically significant may be zero or may be all of them. In Figure 28, there are two: "quickly completed call" and "confidence in solution."

The impact of "quickly completed call" is apparently much larger than the impact of "confidence in solution." Most importantly, the performance on "quickly completed call" is only 72 compared to the 85 for "confidence in solution." As suggested in Figure 18, "quickly completed call" has implications for further system training, or perhaps a system improvement is required. The training is obviously less expensive than a system change, so you may want to begin with the training. If you suspect a system problem and have been attempting to garner support for the upgrade, this information would be valuable to include in the discussion.

The "confidence in solution" attribute is statistically impacting satisfaction and the performance is at the 85% level. This provides the manager with an opportunity to distribute this information about the center. It may become a service differentiator: that is, something around which to build an advertising campaign touting your service as being above that of your competitors.

The next figure suggests that most of our improvement opportunities will stem from improving people, processes, or adding enabling technology.

Uncovering Opportunities

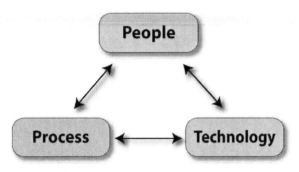

Figure 30: Uncovering opportunities for change initiatives. (Purdue Research Foundation)

The fact is that a focused post-call survey program can help you find what needs to be improved.

The changes made as a result of the CS measurement program should be tracked very carefully. When results from the next measurement period are produced, a comparison of the new results to those in Figures 17 and 18 will enable the success of the actions to be evaluated.

One other way to present the results of the external metrics plotted in Figures 27 and 28 is to place the individual attributes on a matrix as shown in Figure 31. With such a matrix, it becomes immediately possible to see where improvement is needed.

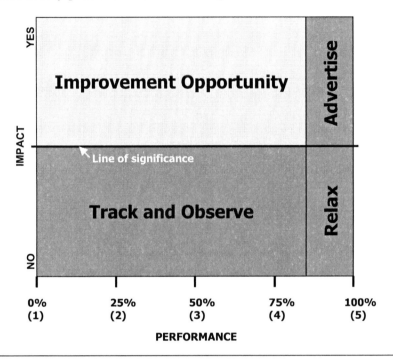

Figure 31: Improvement decision matrix. (Purdue Research Foundation)

Customer-Driven Contact Center Management

The ultimate customer satisfaction improvement method is one that allows the customers to define great service. Every customer has opinions, even when no one asks.

Do you know the impact that your contact center has on your company image? BenchmarkPortal recently contacted 1,000 U.S. consumers to ask them about their experience with contact centers. Ninety-two percent said their experience was important in shaping their image of the company (see Figure 32).

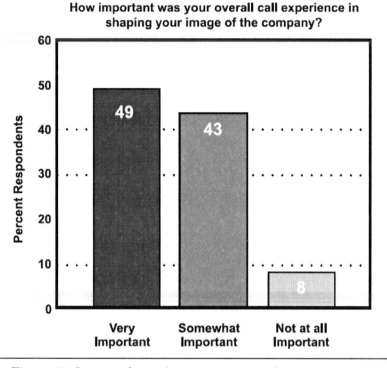

Figure 32: Impact of experience on company image. (Purdue Research Foundation)

In today's global economy, as markets reach higher and higher levels of saturation, new customers become harder to find. The companies that endure are those that ensure their current customers are not just satisfied—but loyal.

Customer Satisfaction Drivers

In the following illustration, customer needs can be summed up as follows:

Anton's Hierarchy of Caller Needs

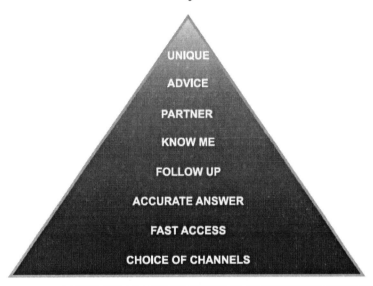

Figure 33: Anton's Hierarchy of Caller Needs. (Purdue Research Foundation)

By drilling down, these needs can be classified into two primary categories:

- **low-value satisfaction drivers:**
  - receiving accurate answers
  - having fast access
  - being offered a choice of contact channels
- **high-value satisfaction drivers:**
  - being treated as unique
  - receiving specific advice
  - regarded as a partner in the company-customer relationship
  - feeling that the company "Knows Me"
  - receiving timely follow-up to their contact

Unfortunately, what many contact centers measure and manage are ...

- accurate answers;
- fast access;
- a choice of contact channels;

...When what they should be focusing on are ...

- treating each customer as unique;
- providing specific advice above and beyond their expectations;
- regarding each customer as a partner in the relationship;
- making the customer feel that the company "Knows Me"; and
- providing timely follow-up to their contact.

Customer Feedback Methods

Sometimes company use a completely passive "suggestion box" approach to customer feedback. As depicted in the next figure, these are not that well used by customers.

Figure 34: Suggestion boxes attract primarily the very angry customers. (Purdue Research Foundation)

Traditional customer satisfaction survey feedback methods have been to periodically contact a randomly selected sample of customers to ask them what they felt about their most recent contact experience. These methods usually involved a delay of anywhere from several days to several weeks, thus relying upon the memory of the customer.

While these methods have honorable intentions (and are certainly better than having no formal method for gathering customer feedback), they are flawed in that there is a distinct disconnect between the contact event and the conduct of the survey. Thus, although the feedback is still somewhat useful as a temperature gauge of customer satisfaction, the value of being able to use their feedback to implement immediate improvements in contact handling, training, and coaching is diminished.

The best methods of customer feedback gathering involve asking the customer to respond to a satisfaction survey immediately, as soon as their reason for contact has been satisfied. Immediate feedback enables management to take positive steps to address any negative feedback while the contact experience is fresh on the mind of the agent, and permits management to investigate whether there exists systemic issues that should be addressed.

Briefly, here is a summary of the most common types of customer satisfaction survey methods.

> ***Post-call (agent-initiated)*** – At the conclusion of a call, the caller is asked if he/she would be willing to answer a few short questions regarding their feelings about their "just-completed" calling experience. If they answer affirmatively, the caller is immediately connected to an IVR where scripted questions are asked and their responses are recorded and automatically tabulated. Daily reports are then generated and distributed to management for any follow-up actions that may be indicated.

Post-call (fully automated) – Before the call begins, an IVR asks the caller if they would participate in a post-call survey. If the caller says "yes," the survey is either fielded automatically after the call (auto-route into the IVR), or immediately after the caller hangs up, an auto-dialer re-calls the caller to field the survey (Outbound IVR Survey). This re-dial occurs within seconds.

Post- email – Similar to Post-call surveys, Post-email survey invitations are appended to email responses asking the customer to click on a link to complete a short survey regarding their customer service experience. Clicking on the link connects the customer to an automated email questionnaire which presents a few short multiple-choice questions related to the email response they received. Their responses are automatically tabulated. Daily reports are then generated and distributed to management for any follow-up actions that may be indicated.

Post-chat – Post-chat surveys essentially follow the same form and process as Post-email surveys outlined above.

Post-Web self-service – As with Post-chat surveys, these surveys follow the same form and process as Post-email surveys.

The table on the next page shows a cross section of survey fielding (collections) methods and how they stack up against each other.

Table 2: Comparison of survey fielding methods. (Purdue Research Foundation)

Method	Agree to take survey	Cost Factor	Cost per Survey	Agent Aware?	Agent Level Feedback?	Best Solution Combining Factors
Phone Survey	20 - 40%		$8-$25	No	No	Special Cases
Email Survey	15 - 30%		50¢ or less	No	Yes	Highly Recommended
Auto-Route into IVR after call	20 - 30%		$2.00 - $4.00	No	Yes	Sometimes Recommended
Agent Transfer into Survey	30 - 50%		50¢ - $1.50	Yes	Yes/No	Sometimes Recommended
Outbound IVR Survey	20 - 30%		80¢ - $1.75	No	Yes	Highly Recommended

As you can see there are differences between each of these survey fielding methods. The authors are partial to either the agent-initiated IVR survey (less costly to implement), or the automated outbound IVR survey (a little more costly to implement, but offers the best overall results).

The next table on survey fielding methods adds a few more data points for decision-making.

Table 3: Survey fielding method comparisons (Purdue Research Foundation)

Characteristics	IVR Survey	Telephone	E-mail
Avg. Lag Time	5 seconds	30 Hours	24 hours
Avg. Response Rate	20 – 30 %	20 – 40 %	15 – 30 %
Data Entry Errors	Low	Medium	Low
Survey Cycle Time	4 hours	30 Days	24 hours
Cost/3 minute survey (numeric only)	$0.50 - $1.25	$18.00	$0.50
Cost /3 minute survey (numeric w/one open ended question)	$0.75 - $1.95	$22.00	$0.50

Here again, we see that the post-call IVR survey has a lot of advantages, but we want to emphasize that if you have your caller's email address, that overall, this survey fielding methods has the greatest range of advantages in terms of implementation, operations, effectiveness, and costs.

Automating the Customer Feedback Process

A widely used option for collecting customer satisfaction data is the use of an automated voice-response or automated e-mail - response system survey process. Immediately upon completion of the contact, a predetermined sample of your customers is automatically transferred to the automated survey system. The automated system plays the survey introduction in a recorded human voice or scripted e-mail and begins asking the survey questions. The system waits for the customer to speak, touch-tone key or type their answer to evaluate each service aspect using a 1-5 or a 1-10 scale. The system essentially operates as if it were a "live-agent" interviewer.

The following figure shows the call flow of an automated post-call survey methodology.

Post-Call Survey Flow Chart

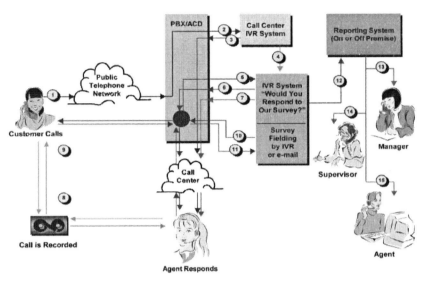

Figure 35: Post-call IVR survey flow chart (Purdue Research Foundation)

The use of automated survey technology raises a question for contact center managers. How will our customers react to an automated survey? In response to this question, we conducted a test to compare the standard telephone interview methodology with an automated survey system.

Customers to an inbound customer service center were contacted 24 to 72 hours later by an interviewer or immediately after the initial contact by the automated survey system and asked to complete a customer satisfaction survey. In total, 401 customers participated in the survey for a 44% participation rate, compared to 452 callers and a 66% participation rate for the automated survey method.

67

To further explore customer reaction to the automated survey, we asked customers to rate the acceptability of the survey they had just completed on a scale of 1 to 10 with 1 the lowest. Their responses fell into the categories shown in Figure 36.

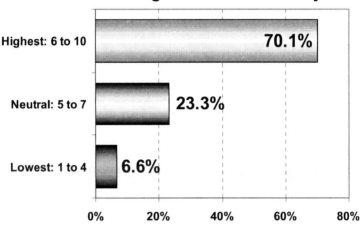

Customer Rating of Automated Survey

Figure 36. Customer rating of automated survey (Purdue Research Foundation)

Gathering customer perception data using an automated system has several advantages over the more commonly used telephone and mail survey formats:

1. There is considerably less expense per survey.

2. A statistically representative sample at the 95% confidence level can always be collected due to the lower cost per survey.

3. Customer opinions are more accurate because the evaluation occurs immediately or nearly immediately after the initial customer service experience.

4. The customer who experienced the service is always the one to compete the survey.

5. Survey data entry costs are eliminated since the customer enters the data.

6. Errors are significantly reduced if not eliminated altogether.

7. Actual customer comments are recorded verbatim and can be listened to or reviewed and referred to afterwards.

8. Internal metrics can be collected at the same time as the automated survey allowing direct statistical correlation between internal and external metrics.

9. Survey cycle time (period of interest being measured which includes the data collection period + report generation) is considerably shorter.

10. Data can be turned into management information almost immediately.

Using automated surveys can reduce your cost and increase the value of your customer satisfaction program. The automated survey system is an exciting tool for quality of service measurement and contact center management.

Driving Customer Feedback into Action and Change

Gathering customer feedback is the first step in managing customer relationships, but it mustn't stop there. This is part of a continuous customer satisfaction improvement cycle that involves not only customer opinions, but agent behavior, service recovery, and failed service analysis.

The four main components of a solution to drive customer feedback into action and behavioral change are:

1. Customer Opinion

- Direct, focused questions
- Collected by e-mail or after-call IVR survey
- Details by customer type

- Drill down by reason for contact
- Details of why dissatisfied

2. Agent Behavior

- Based on best practice findings
- Metrics aligned with true objectives
- Unfiltered feedback directly from the customers they served

3. Service Recovery

- Provides instant damage control of dissatisfied customers
- Recovery done by key recovery talent
- Tracks impact of various recovery methods
- Management has details on service break-downs
- Customers resurveyed to ensure final satisfaction

4. Failed Service Analysis

- Easy-to-read reporting of drivers of dissatisfaction
- Unbiased details from customers
- Impact versus performance charts
- Trending information on impact initiatives
- Determine effectiveness of products, policies, and processes

The following figure (also the cover of the book) depicts the "big picture" of interpreting customer data into actionable reports.

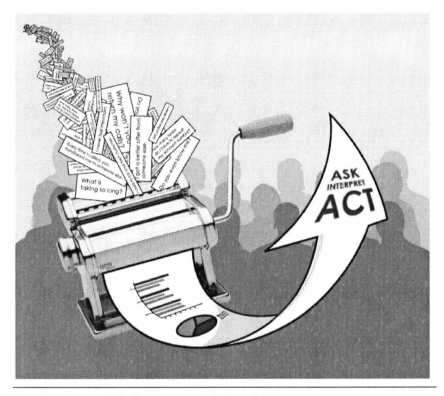

Figure 37: Ask, Interpret, and then ACT. (Purdue Research Foundation)

Caller feedback survey results are processed and reported to agents, supervisors, and management on a continuous "dashboard basis". The following are just a few examples of the reports available in a world-class caller feedback system for agents.

**Agents get real-time feedback from
the customers they served**

Agent Dashboard

Today is 03/10/2005

26 days	Percent Top Box	Percent Satisfaction Score	Absolute Satisfaction Score	Percent Neutral Score	Percent Dissatisfied Score	Percent Very Dissatisfied Score	Percent Resolved	Click For More Info
Overall	53.12%	84.37%	4.31	9.37%	6.25%	2%	100.00%	32 Surveys

Scores do not include surveys considered 'staging'

More Information ✕

Options:	Compared to Queue ▼		From:	Select Date Range	Report This Score: Top Box ▼	Go!
Queue:	List of Surveys	All...	To:		Efficient ▼	

*Figure 38: A classic agent dashboard where all the metrics critical
for self-management are shown. (Purdue Research Foundation)*

**Best Practice Study showed
self-directed learning is
longest lasting...**

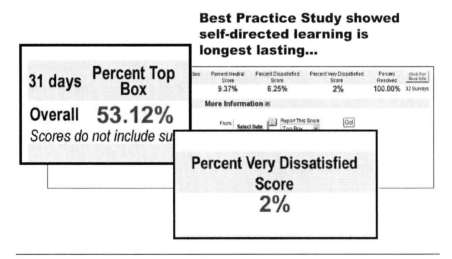

*Figure 39: Top box indicating the percent of perfect scores is shown
along with bottom box which indicates the percent of the lowest scores.
(Purdue Research Foundation)*

Agents instantly see how they compare

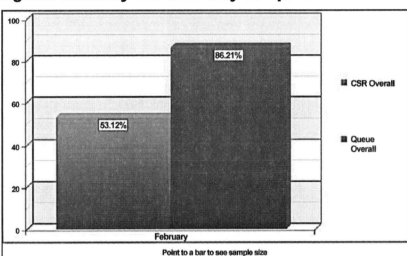

Figure 40: The agent can compare their top box performance with that of others in the same queue and see that they are underperforming. (Source: ECHO™ Reports)

This self-evaluation can encourage the agent to begin self-management steps such as:

- Review their recorded calls to better understand the reason for their poor performance;

- Drill down to observe trends in their own performance; and

- Ask their supervisor to evaluate their performance and give advice.

Ranking

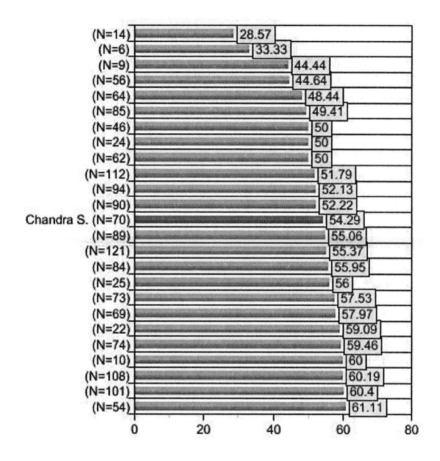

Figure 41: Ranking Chart (Source: ECHO™ Reports)

In drilling down for more information, the agent can quickly see that they are in "the middle of the pack" regarding top box performance. For most individuals, this would bring on the question, "why am performing in such an average way, maybe I should ask for some coaching."

Performance vs Queue

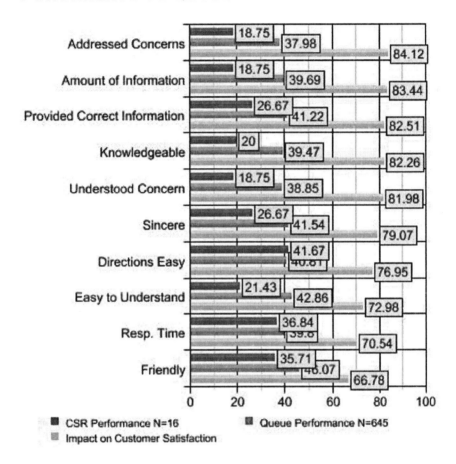

Figure 42: Performance vs. Queue Chart (Source: ECHO™ Reports)

In this report, the agent can quickly see not only their performance relative to the queue on all attributes, but also the impact that attribute's performance has on their over-all satisfaction score. In this report, the agent can quickly deduce that they need to improve on "addressing the caller's concerns."

The next set of figures are examples of supervisor reports.

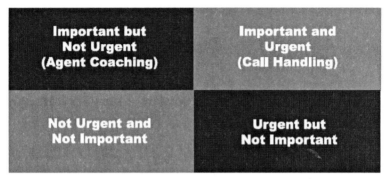

Supervisor Time-Management Quadrants

Source: Stephen Covey

Figure 43: Supervisor time-management quadrants

First we want to emphasize that a contact center supervisor is mostly focused on ensuring that there are ample resources to handle all incoming calls. This is their "urgent and important" quadrant. Though they are aware of the importance of coaching, they also know that there is often not enough time to get the job done (important but not urgent activity). Therefore, having reports that help the supervisor focus on the agents in most need of their coaching are essential.

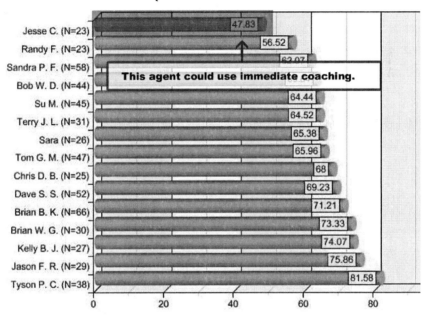

Rank performance for all Agents
- Top Box Satisfaction -

Figure 44: Ranking performance of all agents. (Source: ECHO™ Reports)

This report ranks the supervisor's agents by top box performance. If limited by time on a particular day, the supervisor can decide to spend time coaching the agent in most need of help. In this case, that would be Jesse.

Rank performance for all Agents

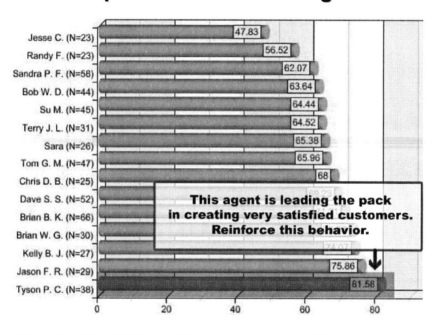

Figure 45: Ranking performance of all agents. (Source: ECHO™ Reports)

This report immediately pin-points the top performing agent, whose performances needs to be noted and appreciated. If time limited, the supervisor could ask Jesse to monitor and observe the performance of Tyson to learn in the process.

The next set of figures are examples of manager reports.

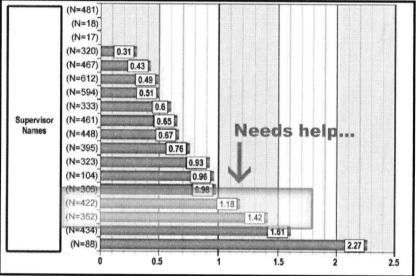

Figure 46: Bottom box performance ranked by supervisors. (Source: ECHO™ Reports)

All busy contact center managers need actionable reports that allow them to focus where they are most needed. In this case, the manager would focus on the supervisor whose total average bottom box scores are the highest, indicating poor performance.

Compare the distribution of scores by team, by queue, by supervisor, by location...and more

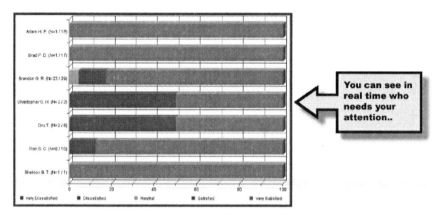

Figure 47: Team performance comparisons by team. (Source: ECHO™ Reports)

At the click of a mouse, the manager can compare performance by team, by queue, by supervisor, by location, and more. This on-line and ad hoc "management by the numbers" allows managers to constantly and in real-time manage their contact center for optimum performance.

Compare the distribution of scores by team, by queue, by supervisor, by location...and more

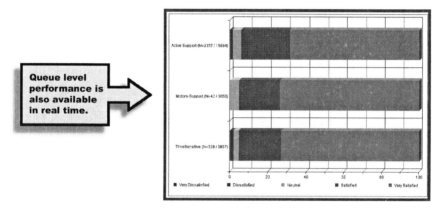

Figure 48: Team performance comparisons by queue. (Source: ECHO™ Reports)

81

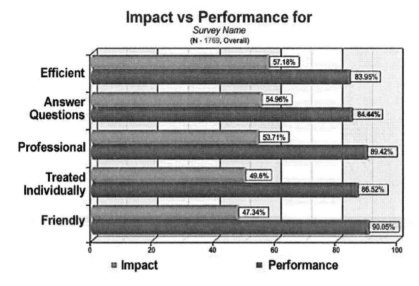

Figure 49: Impact versus performance comparisons. (Source: ECHO™ Reports)

A constant focus by contact center managers is "where to apply improvement initiatives?" This report shows immediately that the one attribute that has the highest impact on overall satisfaction and the lowest performance by the agents in total is "efficiently answering the callers' questions and/or handling their issues." This discovery then warrants initiating a training program that would improve this area of performance.

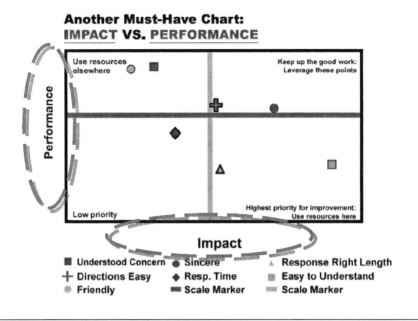

Figure 50: Impact versus performance matrix. (Purdue Research Foundation)

This one report actually has all of the information that a contact center managers needs to take action. First of all, recognize that it includes all attributes being evaluated by the survey process. Secondly, notice that the x-axis is "impact" on overall satisfaction, whereas the y-axis is the overall performance of all of the center's agents. Each quadrant has its own obvious actionable instructions, namely:

upper right =	"keep up the good work on these attributes";
upper left =	"you're overdoing these attributes....use resources elsewhere";
lower left =	"low priority" attributes, i.e., do nothing;
lower right =	"highest priority for improvement"...so use your resources here to improve results.

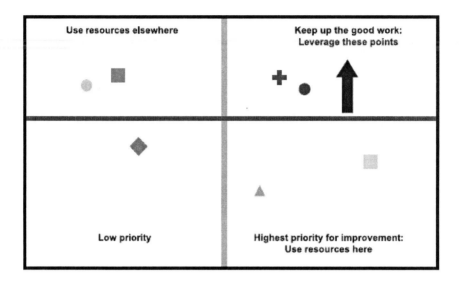

Figure 51: This is an enlargement of the impact-performance matrix. (Purdue Research Foundation)

This is merely an enlargement of the previous figure, and shows which attributes to leverage.

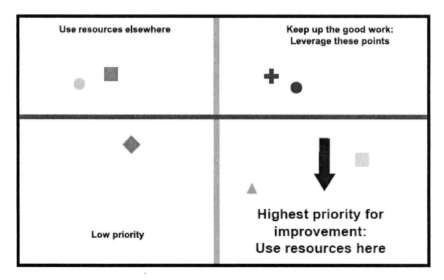

Figure 52: This is an enlargement of the impact-performance matrix. (Purdue Research Foundation)

This is merely an enlargement of the previous figure, and shows which attributes are the highest priority for improvement.

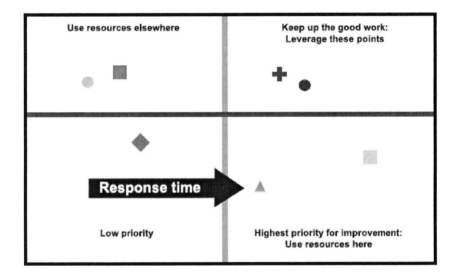

Figure 53: This is an enlargement of the impact-performance matrix. (Purdue Research Foundation)

So, jumping out of this report is the message to the contact center manager, "begin an initiative for improving response time...this is your highest priority"!!!

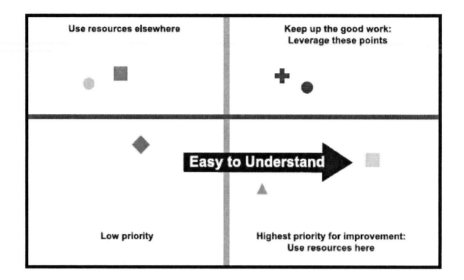

Figure 54: This is an enlargement of the impact-performance matrix. (Purdue Research Foundation)

So, jumping out of this report is the message to the contact center manager, "begin an initiative for improving 'easy of understand'...this is your second highest priority"...

The next figures are examples of reports for the training department,

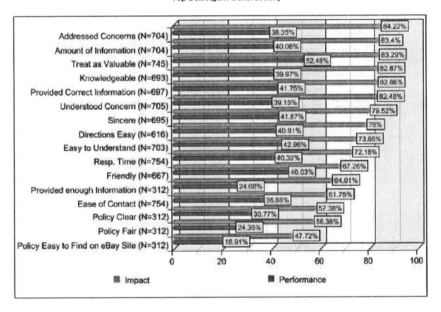

Impact vs Performance for
('Active Billing')
Top Box Agent Satisfaction)

Figure 55: Impact versus performance by queue. (Source: ECHO™ Reports)

In a caller feedback system, it is also important that the training department manager can access where the "weak spots" are in the training program. This ranking report indicates that training needs to address more thoroughly the aspect of "addressing the caller's concerns."

For All Records

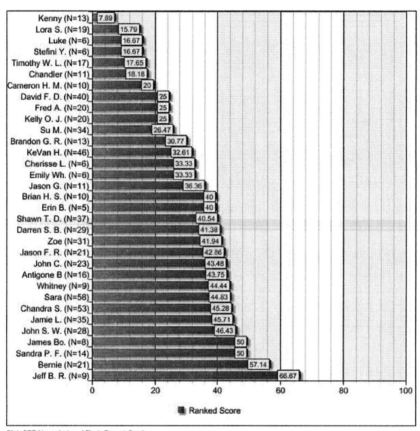

Figure 56: Ranking by queue by agent. (Source: ECHO™ Reports)

Here the training department manager can easily pick out those individual in most need for training on the attribute of "addressing the caller's concerns."

Key Performance Indicators of Success

Which CRM center KPIs correlate best to customer satisfaction? The KPI most predictive of a positive customer satisfaction is "first time final," or "first/final" (see Figure 57). This term refers to the percentage of caller issues handled completely on the first call. This KPI measures the ability of a call center to answer a caller's question or solve a caller's problem on the first call without a transfer or callback. The key performance indicator most predictive of negative customer satisfaction is error rate. This is the number of input errors per 1,000 entries.

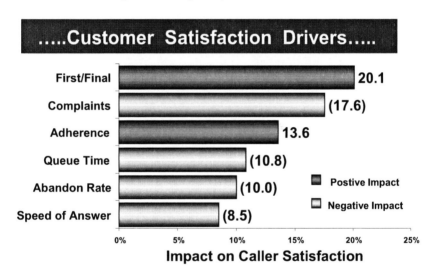

Source: Purdue University Research (published in *Call Center Magazine* July 2001)

Figure 57: The top six KPIs that drive customer satisfaction

The way this was determined was to list all KPIs that could affect customer satisfaction (see Table 4). Then each KPI was evaluated to determine which of these was the best indicator of positive and negative customer satisfaction.

What is the statistical relationship of each KPI to customer satisfaction? This is best answered by the graph shown in Figure 58. This graph shows that customer satisfaction is linearly related to improvements in the KPI known as "first/final." The relationship of each KPI to customer satisfaction was further correlated, and examples are given in tables 5 and 6. For example, the KPIs that drive customer satisfaction versus the function of the call center are shown in Table 5.

Another example of the KPIs that drive customer satisfaction in various industries is shown in Table 6. What is important to notice here is that a KPI that drives customer satisfaction in one type of call center is not the same KPI that best measures customer satisfaction in another. This is why you cannot use another company's strategy, technology choices, or KPIs. All of this must be determined based on what your company's business strategy aims to accomplish. And this is why, when one CEO says, "We need CRM!" it does not mean the same solution will fit another company's needs. Each company has to create its own, unique solution based on the CEO's business strategy, the most important customer segments, and the plan in our Magic Squares.

Table 4: All KPIs That Could Affect Customer satisfaction (Purdue Research Foundation)

KPIs for Customer satisfaction
Percentage of first time final calls (first/final)
Percent agent turnover (turnover)
Percent abandonment (abandon)
Percent attendance (attendance)
Percent agent occupancy (occupancy)
Percent adherence to schedule (adherence)
Service level (service level)
Calls handled per 8-hour shift (calls per shift)
Base salary (base salary)
Average talk time (talk time)
Cubicle space (cubicle space)
Input errors per 1,000 records (error rate)
Ratio of supervisors to agents (ratio agent/super)
Time in queue (queue time)
Average after-call work time (after call work time)
Initial training time (training time)
Percent calls blocked (calls blocked)
Average cost to hire a new agent (new agent cost)
Cost per call (cost per call)
Hourly salary (hourly salary)
Percent complaints regarding previous call (complaints)

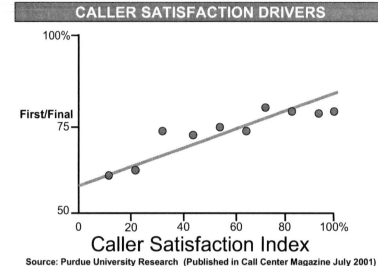

Figure 58: Customer satisfaction is linearly related to improvements in the KPI known as "first/final".

Table 5: KPIs for Call Centers with Different Functions (Purdue Research Foundation)

Technical Products Call Centers:
Positive Impact on CSI
Hourly salary
Cost per call
Hiring costs
Negative Impact on CSI
Complaints
Calls blocked
Call Routing Calls Centers:
Positive Impact on CSI
Speed of answer
Hiring costs
Attendance
Ration of agents/supers
Negative Impact on CSI
Complaints

Table 6: The KPIs in Different Industries (Purdue Research Foundation)

Technical Products Call Centers:
Positive Impact on CSI
Training time
Hourly salary
Ratio of agents/supers
After call work time
Negative Impact
Abandon
Financial Services Call Centers:
Positive Impact on CSI
First/final
Training time
Speed of answer
Service levels
Negative Impact
Queue time
Insurance Call Centers:
Positive Impact on CSI
First/final
Training time
Adherence
Negative Impact on CSI
Calls blocked
Turnover

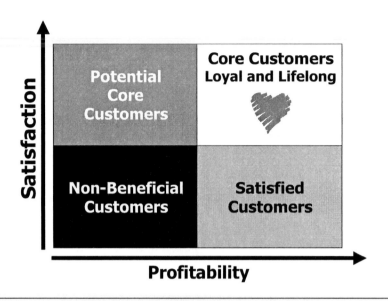

Figure 59: Customer differentiation and contribution to profitability. (Purdue Research Foundation)

CHAPTER 6: SERVICE RECOVERY

The Process of Service Recovery

What Angry People Need and Want

When you have dealt with an angry customer, you may have asked yourself "What does this person want from me?", or even perhaps asked the customer this question. It is an important question that has a number of answers. Knowing the answers will help you calm down an angry person, and reduce hostile behavior directed at you.

They Want What They Want

The most obvious answer to the question is customers want their problem solved. That is, if they contact you expecting to receive help, they want that help. Or, if they call to talk to a particular person, they want to speak to that person now.

In other words, the customer interacts with your company with a particular goal in mind. Unfortunately, we cannot always do what the customer wants, since we have to work within the constraints of our jobs. We don't always have the authority, or even the ability to meet the requests of clients.

So, most of the time we can't give them what they ask for. If clients only "wanted what they wanted" we would have little chance of calming them down, since we can't always accommodate them. Luckily, there are some psychological needs that you can address. Fulfill these needs and you will reduce hostile behavior.

They Want Help

Angry or hostile people want you to be helpful, even if you can't solve their entire problem. If they see you as making a genuine effort on their behalf, they are much less likely to be hostile towards you personally. Think about your own experience for a moment. Have you ever had the experience of going into a department store to make a purchase? You walked in and had difficulty finding the item you wanted? After searching throughout the store, you finally find a staff person. When you ask the employee where you might find the widgets, you get a response like this:

"Don't know. That's not my department. "

Infuriating isn't it? Why do we get angry in this situation? Sure, it's aggravating that we can't find the item. But what really sends us through the roof is the lack of helpfulness shown by the staff member.

If the employee had said . . .

"Golly, I don't know, but if you wait a moment I can find out."

. . . that would be an entirely different story. We would appreciate the effort being made for us, and be less likely to harass the employee making the effort.

The same goes for your customers. When you make an effort, or appear to be trying to help, your customers are less likely to strike out at you.

They Want Choices

Your clients want to feel they have choices and alternatives. They do not want to feel helpless, or trapped, or at the mercy of the "system". The analogy I like is that of an animal that is cornered. If its only way of escaping is through you, you can be pretty sure that it is going to attack you with great energy. The same is true of your clients. Make them feel they have no options, or they are trapped, and they will tend to strike out at you, even if they are the authors of their own misfortune.

On the other hand, offer choices whenever possible, and you are less likely to be attacked by the upset individual.

Let's look at a simple example.

You answer the phone and the caller asks to speak to Jessica Jones. Ms. Jones is out of the office at the moment. You say:

"I'm sorry but Ms. Jones is away from her desk at the moment. I will take a message and she will call you back."

That's not a bad response, but note that it offers the caller no choice. Now look at another possibility.

Angry or hostile people want you to be helpful, even if you can't solve their entire problem. If they see you as making a genuine effort on their behalf, they are much less likely to be hostile towards you, such as:

"I'm sorry but Ms. Jones is away from her desk. Would you like her to call you back at a particular time, or would you prefer to call again after 3:00, when she will be available?"

Much better. The difference is subtle. The first response offers no option, but the second allows the caller to choose, or in fact to suggest some other possibility that might be workable. The second example is much less likely to set the customer "off".

There are always choices to offer. And we know that customers respond positively to being offered choices. It reduces their sense of helplessness.

They Want Acknowledgment

Perhaps one of the most important things an angry person wants is to be acknowledged. People want to feel you are making the effort to understand their situation, and their emotional reactions to it. Often, the simple act of acknowledging that a person is upset will help to calm them down, provided the acknowledgment is phrased and "toned" correctly.

The most common error public servants make when dealing with an angry client is to ignore the feelings being expressed, and shift immediately into a problem-solving mode. Unfortunately, customers perceive this approach as uncaring, unfeeling, and unhelpful, thus intensifying their anger.

It is critically important that you acknowledge the emotions being expressed. Later, when we talk about specific techniques and phrases, we will explain how to use empathy and active listening as ways of acknowledging the person's feelings.

To summarize, angry customers want you to fix their problem, but often this just isn't possible. Luckily, they also want ...

- helpfulness and effort on your part ;

- to feel they have choices; and

- acknowledgment of their situation and their feelings.

By recognizing these "wants", and providing for them, you can have a significant impact on the degree of hostility directed at you.

Managing a Customer Recovery Process

Having respect for your customers will ensure their faith in and loyalty to you and your business. Studies show that it is nine times more difficult to attract a new customer than it is to retain an existing one, so it is critical to keep your customers happy. Surveys, focus groups and questionnaires are among the ways to measure your customers' perceptions of you and determine how to improve.

Here are a couple of actionable reports in the service recover process.

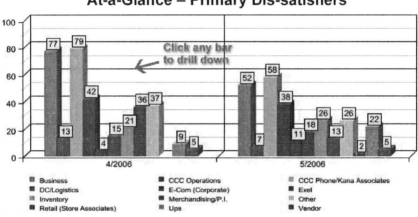

Figure 60: At a glance the primary "dis-satisfiers". (Source: ECHO™ Reports)

From the chart, the service recovery team can see the trends by months…in this case for two months. It appears that the highest incident of service issues for both months is "inventory," making it clear that we want to "drill down" on this data to find out why.

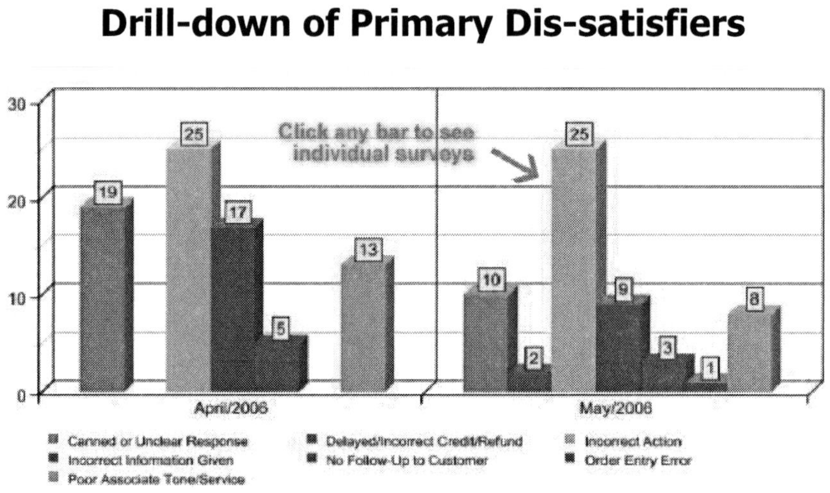

Drill-down of Primary Dis-satisfiers

Figure 61: Inventory issues. (Source: ECHO™ Reports)

By investigating the "inventory issues," it becomes immediately clear that the real culprit here is specifically "incorrect action" taken by the agent population. This is a training issue and easily corrected now that it is so pointedly discovered. A perfect example of ask, interpret, and then action.

If you discover that a customer is dissatisfied, take action immediately to win back their confidence in the services you provide. People like to know that their opinion counts and if they feel like you care about what they think, they will think positive thoughts about you and your business.

Managing Upset Customers

Here's a 60 second guide on how to manage upset customers and turn them into long-term, satisfied customers.

0:60   Stay Calm

Listen carefully to your customers' complaints without interrupting. Acknowledge that there is a problem and empathize with upset customers. Let them know what you can do for them and make them aware of all of their options. Always treat your customers with respect. Customers should sense that you are calm, but concerned. Your attitude when dealing with upset customers should be professional, mature, pleasant and reasonable.

0:46   Work at Gaining Loyal Customers

The number one reason that customers stop buying from a business is because they were treated poorly by someone. It is much more cost effective to retain loyal customers than to gain new ones. In order to create loyalty, you have to calm down upset customers and ensure them that you will work to find a solution that they deem acceptable. Let them know that their business is important. Thank them for their patience and cooperation. In many cases, it pays to reward upset customers in order to keep their business.

0:38   Look & Act Professional

A first impression is a lasting impression. Your appearance should signal that you are professional, mature and knowledgeable. Nonverbal communication also says a lot. Your body language and tone of voice should be polite and tactful. Pay attention to your facial expressions, posture, gestures and speech.

0:20   Choose Who You Want to Do Business With

There are some people who will never be happy with
your products or services. Repeated complaints from a
customer and terminal dissatisfaction are signs that you
cannot please him or her. Your business is better off
without such customers and you may want to refer them
elsewhere.

0:11   Ensure that Mistakes Aren't Repeated

Once you determine the problem and how it originated,
you can take steps to ensure that it does not happen
again. Learning about a problem can actually help
improve your business if you make sure that the
problem is avoided in the future. Don't make the same
mistake twice. In dealing with upset customers, you also
learn about human behavior and become better at
resolving similar situations in the future.

0:03   Don't Take Criticism Personally

Many discourteous customers act that way because they
made a mistake and want to blame someone else. Don't
let these customers get to you by responding
emotionally or giving in to outrageous demands. Tears,
anger and sarcasm are inappropriate reactions. (24)

CHAPTER 7: CUSTOMER BEHAVIOR ANALYTICS

Analyzing the Survey

We have finally reached the stage in the customer satisfaction measurement process that everyone looks forward to — the actual analysis of data and interpretation of reports. We will discuss several types of analyses in this section and explain why we recommend certain approaches. Some statistical terms are used to explain various types of output, and both the terms and the output are explained in the text. Even if you have no background in statistics, almost all this material should be easily grasped. You should think about the purpose of each technique and how it might be used in your organization rather than just about the specifics of the statistical output.

In this section, we will be using generic examples of customer satisfaction analysis. We do this so that the focus is primarily on the technique being illustrated and its interpretation rather than on a particular business or industry. We have also chosen a moderate-sized sample of about 500 respondents for analysis because many customer satisfaction surveys are about this size. The tables in this section were generated by the SPSS statistical software product.

Preliminary Analyses

Before beginning any heavy-duty analysis, we recommend exploring the data to look for interesting patterns, odd cases and outlying values. If you find them, it can mean one of several things — bad data, an unexpected phenomenon or a unique group of customers. Knowing these possible pitfalls will improve your analysis and reporting.

Preparing For Comprehensive Analysis

To better prepare for the analysis, keep the following principles in mind.

- Rare events often drive the satisfaction processes, such as a poor experience with an unfriendly employee or one bad meal in a restaurant.

- Just as critical are unresolved problems that can dominate perceptions, such as the time when an airline lost and couldn't find a passenger's luggage, then provided inadequate reimbursement. In terms of the model, attribute importance and expectation effects would be dominated by the experiences/problems variable in determining both attribute and overall satisfaction. Severe problems can lead to direct paths from the problems variable to the overall satisfaction and willingness to repurchase and recommend variables.

There are "pull" factors as well. These are best measured in terms of attribute importance. For example, many people go to a hospital because it has a reputation for having very good doctors. The pull then is the importance placed upon a quality medical staff in combination with expectations. The "push" factors are the actual experiences and problems (often rare events, as just spelled out), in combination with those same expectations.

Most people are satisfied with your products and services or else they wouldn't still be customers. Focus more on those with negative attitudes and lower levels of satisfaction to understand how to increase satisfaction (and to get feedback through the surveying program).

Statistical Analysis

Many people are intimidated by statistical analysis procedures and believe they will never understand what is going on or grasp what it means. It is important to note what the term analysis means. It is the "separation or breaking up of a whole into its fundamental elements or component parts; a detailed examination of anything complex made in order to understand its nature or to determine its essential features" (Webster's Third New World International Dictionary). Statistical analysis performs these functions. Essentially all statistical analysis is data reduction; that is, it seeks to reduce the mass of the data down to meaningful subsets. Additionally, statistical analysis is used to make it easier to understand what the subsets mean.

It is not necessary to understand the formula or even to see it in order to use it and use it well. Just as we do not need to be chemists with an understanding of the effects of heat on various food chemicals in order to prepare a satisfying meal, so can we use statistical software to analyze data and create actionable reports without understanding why statisticians chose the exact form of the formula in use.

You will, however, need to acquire a little vocabulary. Specifically we will discuss six types of errors, four types of data, three measures of central tendency, the concept of statistical significance and its relationship to practical or substantive significance, and individual vs. summary level analysis.

In Appendix A, two case studies are presented to further illustrate these statistical analysis concepts.

Continuous Improvement in the Customer Satisfaction Process

Many people believe that there is little use in "re-inventing the wheel." But the customer satisfaction process needs to be dynamic in order to respond to the ever-changing environment.

Once You Start You Can't Stop

We hope that we do not have to "sell" you on the importance of keeping the program going once you have it started; it may, however, be necessary to convince someone else. Just remember that even though at times management may appear ready to cut the customer satisfaction surveying program, it does not necessarily mean they want to do so. Maybe they just need you to provide them with a strong justification for the program. You will be able to do that best if you have carefully tracked what has been learned and implemented as a result of the customer satisfaction surveying program. Reflect back on linking customer satisfaction to the bottom line and the importance of customer lifetime value. Also it is easier to maintain a program than to stop it and periodically re-start it.

Note that it is critical to continually review the program, its goals and instruments. Chances are that not all aspects of all the products and services made by the company could be included in the first survey. "Optimize" one product or service or one family of products or services and check to see that the desired effect was achieved by re-surveying. Then place the program's major focus on another product or service and reduce the number of questions about the first. In this way, you will be able to provide continuing value to the company.

How Often Should Surveys Be Conducted?

Of all the questions you might have, this is both one of the simplest and most difficult to answer. It is simple to answer because in a stable business, once a year might be enough. In a very complex and changing environment, once a quarter might be insufficient. Survey results can be very valuable, but conducting surveys cannot be done "on the cheap." If an organization can only afford to do one study per year, then that is all that will likely be done.

Management at a company may decide that they would like quarterly customer satisfaction reports, just as they now receive quarterly financials. This is fine if funds and personnel are available to administer the surveys, but in some businesses, results from the survey cannot be used to change the quality of the product or service that rapidly. In other words, customer satisfaction program principles may dictate that surveys are either required more or less often depending upon how quickly change can be implemented.

A product that has been newly introduced, especially in an industry with frequent customer buying decisions, merits more frequent surveys. For instance, when a fast food restaurant chain introduces a new type of hamburger, the company shouldn't wait more than a few days to gauge customer reaction because people have so many choices for fast food dining, and the company must be aware of any changes that must be made in its own offerings to stay competitive.

Creating Internal and External Benchmark Metrics

A comprehensive customer satisfaction surveying system attempts to place measurement sensors at every important moment-of-truth (MOT) event where a customer might experience the performance of your product or service. Consider a measurement approach to each critical MOT as shown in Figure 62. Define the MOT (for instance a phone call from a customer) and then determine what both the internal metrics (see Table 4) and external metrics might be that you can use to drive the results back into process management in order to produce change.

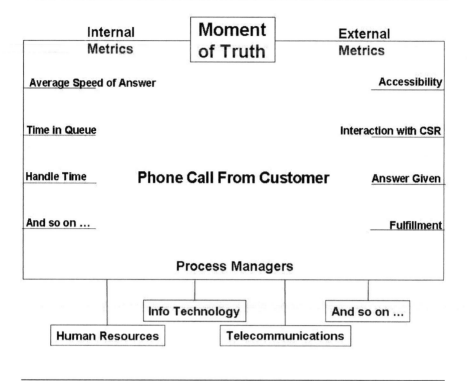

Figure 62: Measuring the Moment of Truth. (Purdue Research Foundation)

External metrics are those attributes that we ask the customer to rate us on through survey fielding and analysis.

Survey results can:

- Help you set current benchmark metrics, i.e., how healthy is the organization currently?
- Help set future goals, i.e., how much should we increase satisfaction by next year at this time?

Given the discussions in various sections about error in surveys, no single survey should be used to set benchmark metrics, and certainly not to set goals that are tied to employee compensation. This is particularly true if the organization is new to customer satisfaction surveying research and therefore using an untested questionnaire.

Both realistically and practically, one of the first quality measures that you can undertake is to continually improve the questionnaires being used in satisfaction measurement. Although questions can't be changed extensively without making comparison from one time period to another problematic, a questionnaire used for the first or second time should be carefully reviewed to look for problems of any type.

It can be a good idea to use focus groups to validate the results of surveys; however, note that focus groups are composed of a small number of people whose individual opinions may or may not exactly match the opinions as expressed on surveys. Caution is urged in evaluating focus group data as well as survey data.

The greatest potential value of focus groups is in uncovering areas that were not considered for inclusion in prior surveys but should be. Problems are often in the eye of the beholder and, if the problem is not apparent to any member of management or the survey team, the opportunities that could exist if the problem were addressed will be missed. We now return our attention to surveys.

Once more than one survey has been completed (at whatever interval is appropriate for your business) the results will provide external benchmark metrics for overall satisfaction, attribute quality ratings, willingness to buy, and most importantly, the occurrence of problems (or quality of service).

Internal benchmark metrics are also easily identified. For instance, an office supply company might link satisfaction to shipping time. An order entry department might link satisfaction to time it takes to process and verify a customer's request. An airline might link overall satisfaction to on-time arrival.

Internal and external benchmarks should be created with the following in mind:

- They must be MOT specific.
- They must be process specific, i.e., relevant to some process manager.
- They must be behaviorally actionable, i.e., within the process manager's ability to change.
- They must be trackable over time.

In general, both internal and external benchmark metrics can be used to:

- Set goals to improve future performance relative to past performance.
- Improve performance relative to competitors.
- Set goals to delight customers by creating products and services to meet customer expectations and requirements.

CHAPTER 8: BUDGETING FOR CUSTOMER FEEDBACK SOLUTIONS

Striving for an All-In-One Solution

Contact center managers want ease of use and reliability in their technology, and would prefer to have one relationship, one vendor, one suite of products, and one common administrative interface. However, many are burdened with legacy "multi-point" solutions that condition their decisions, and some have long-standing relationships with point solution vendors that they want to continue. In addition, others need to be convinced that going with "all-in-one" solution providers will not deprive them of "best-of-breed" excellence, at least for those applications they consider mission-critical to their success.

How managers come out on this issue may have as much to do with their previous experiences, and the perceived weight of their legacy systems, as with the pure operational and financial optimization of their current or future operations.

In a landmark research study conducted in 2006 by BenchmarkPortal, Inc., and sponsored by Interactive Intelligence, their research showed many important distinctions between the two approaches. Some of the key findings from the data allow us to draw the following conclusions:

- Overall, considering all costs, including maintenance costs, establishment of vendor relationships, time required to evaluate new technology, and system administration requirements, the total cost of ownership appears significantly less for an all-in-one solution when compared with its multi-point counter part.

- Administration is more burdensome and requires more resources for multi-point contact centers.

- Integration is sometimes simplified, and the reported ability to leverage the functionality of various applications, is enhanced with all-in-one offerings.

- The ongoing addition of most new technology, applications, and functionality, appears significantly easier for customers who have deployed an all-in-one solution versus those with multi-point products, as shown in the following figure.

Challenges to Adding Technology to Current System

When asked: "Will your current system support planned additions without significant modification or integration issues", 50% said "Yes", while 50% responded "No".

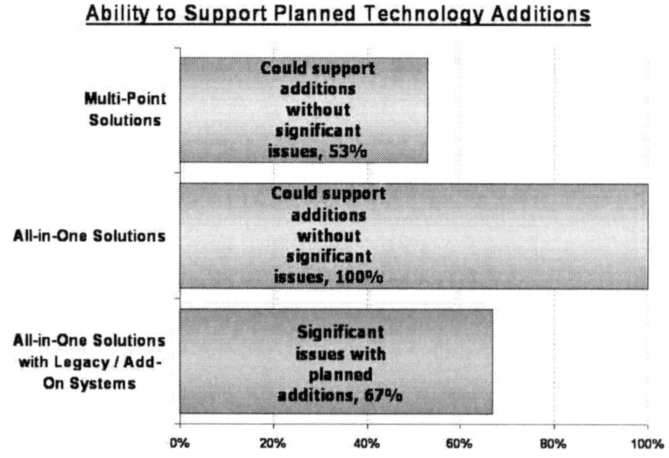

Ability to Support Planned Technology Additions

Figure 63: Ability to support planned technology additions. (Purdue Research Foundation)

112

When the data were cut according to the system type of the respondents, the following insights emerged:

- Fifty-three percent of those with multi-point solutions indicated that their system could support planned additions without significant issues.

- 100% of those with all-in-one solutions said their system could support planned additions without significant issues.

- On the other hand, 67% of centers which had a core all-in-one solution that is weighed down by legacy or add-on systems said they would have significant issues with planned additions.

Thus, while centers with pure all-in-one solutions indicate the easiest path to adding on new functionalities, those with all-in-one solutions plus additional solutions have the hardest time dealing with integration.

As a whole, contact centers recognize the value of reducing the number of vendors they must deal with in the deployment and maintenance of contact center technology.

As part of the research, on-site assessments were conducted at numerous contact centers. The research revealed that the following impact factors were operating in the contact centers visited:

1. **"Cultural Factors"** play a major role in enterprise approaches to technology decisions. That is, the attitudes and experiences with Customer Contact technology that people share in the organization (oftentimes as a result of common experiences, good and bad) create a powerful backdrop against which discussions are framed and decisions are made. People who feel they can handle complexity, customization and integration due to core competencies or past experiences are more likely to favor a multi-point solution approach.

2. **Resource Availability** (aka Budget) varies widely among organizations and has an obvious impact on technology discussions and decisions. Centers studied on-site ranged from one center where the manager was regularly asked if he needed more money, to centers that could only dream of getting the minimum necessary just to hold things together for next year.

3. **Existing IT Systems.** This "legacy factor" is undoubtedly more restricting than it should be in some cases. It is difficult, in the midst of battle, to imagine a world in which familiar screens and trusty old IVRs are tossed out in favor of totally new systems. This is true even where rudimentary ROI analyses and process scenarios might justify the move.

4. **Existing Vendor Relationships.** This is another "legacy factor" and ties into, but is distinguishable from, the previous factor. Where existing vendor relationships have been positive on a personal and a technical level, managers may not feel a need to look at other options, even if budget is not forcing them to stay with legacy systems. In the words of one center manager "we have a good relationship with our vendor. They have been reliable and reasonable and we don't see the need for RFP processes - - nor do we have the time."

5. **Brand Name vs. Completeness of Solution.** Again, this is slightly different than the two previous items. This Impact Factor refers to the fact that oftentimes purchase decisions are made based on the dominance of leading vendors. Customers will often make a "safe" purchase decision by buying from a vendor with high market share, giving less consideration to product factors that are more relevant to the overall success of the contact center. This approach clearly can limit the effectiveness of the purchase decision.

6. **Future Trends.** The need for strategic preparedness is a final Impact Factor that is not shared evenly, however. Certain centers are very focused on getting it right for the long haul, according to a full vision of

where their contact center should be. Others have a more narrow, immediate-term vision. This, too, has an important impact on technology discussions and decisions.

The conclusions drawn from surveys and onsite observations confirmed that assembling and managing a contact center is a very complex business. Getting the right people, processes and technologies all aligned to cultivate loyal customers and build enterprise value is difficult at best.

Against this backdrop, the complexity or simplicity of technology plays an important role in the success and the cost structure of the center. The simpler and more seamless the technology component, the smoother the processes can be and the more effective (and satisfied) the human components can be, all other things being equal. Managers, by and large, consider the advantages and disadvantages of technology against all of the key Technology Process Phases, from specifying solutions through to operation and maintenance of systems.

The voice of the market is clear from the survey. Managers would prefer a single, all-in-one source for all of their technology needs, with a key consideration being that they want that source to provide them with best in class functionality. The participants generally see the all-in-one approach as the trend for the future. In their eyes it has become more attractive over time.

In terms of the future, two items that come out of the study must be mentioned:

1. The current weight of legacy systems, prior experiences and existing vendor relationships will act as drags on migration toward all-in-one solutions; and

2. The all-in-one providers will need to be vigilant in creating, maintaining, and demonstrating best-in-class functionality for all of their offerings.

Considering Off-Premises versus On-Premises Solutions

The breakdown of respondents according to solution type is as follows:

Breakdown of Respondents by Solution Type

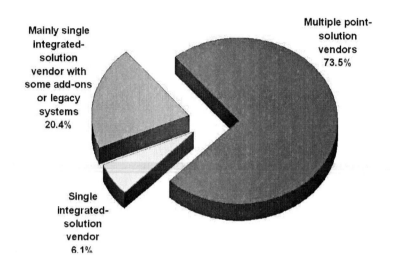

Figure 64: Breakdown of respondents by solution type. (*Purdue Research Foundation*)

These results appear reflective of the industry as a whole. The all-in-one solutions have only been available for 10 years, and have more recently begun to gain significant market share.

Attitudes toward all-in-one platforms seem to reflect mental starting points in the search process, as well as findings on functionality. Consider the following responses, with the first coming from those who purchased multi-point solutions:

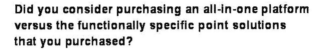

Did you consider purchasing an all-in-one platform versus the functionally specific point solutions that you purchased?

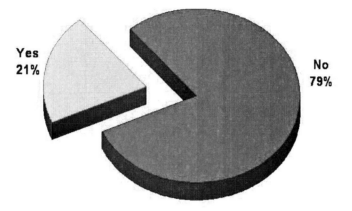

Figure 65: Percentage of respondents that considered an all-in-one platform vs. point solutions. (Purdue Research Foundation)

Thus, only 1 in 5 of those who purchased a multi-point solution even considered an all-in-one solution. Reasons given for this approach included the following text comments:

- IT requirements overrode the business requirements;
- Difficult to adapt legacy systems to all-in-one solutions at the time respondents were shopping;
- Lack of availability of such all-in-one system in the market (at the time we were looking); and
- Multi-point provided best functionality at the time respondents were shopping for it.

The following was obtained from those who purchased an all-in-one platform:

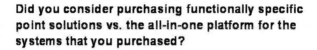

Did you consider purchasing functionally specific point solutions vs. the all-in-one platform for the systems that you purchased?

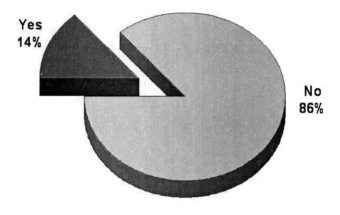

Figure 66: Percentage of respondents that considered functionally specific. point solutions vs. an all-in-one platform. (Purdue Research Foundation)

Thus, 86% of those who purchased an all-in-one solution did not even consider a multi-point solution. The reasons given included the following text comments:

- Easier to administer, and to adapt to change;

- Support is easier and less costly;

- We trust the solutions provider based on long-term relationship; and

- No better single-point solutions available.

Returning now to the survey sample as a whole, we asked about preferences in system type, if all functionalities were available. The overall sentiment was clear:

Given the choice, if you could get all needed functionality from one vendor or multiple vendors, which would you choose?

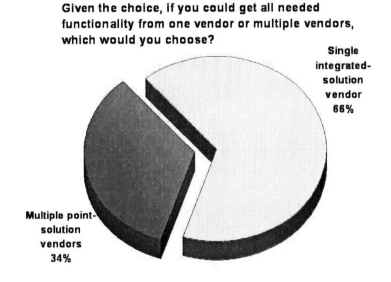

Single integrated-solution vendor 66%

Multiple point-solution vendors 34%

Figure 67: Percentage of respondents that would, given the choice, purchase from a single integrated solutions vendor vs. multi-point solution vendors. (Purdue Research Foundation)

The reasons for preferring an all-in-one solution were made plain during our site visits. The manager of a center with a soft switch all-in-one system said "I have ONE administrator who knows everything. Even better, I have ZERO telecom people. This is heaven compared with my last job."

In another center, management has a hard switch ACD system, but uses the same vendor and VAR for its entire portfolio of technology products, with satisfactory results. From the research, we can conclude that as a whole, contact center customers recognize the value of, and would prefer to work with, a single vendor.

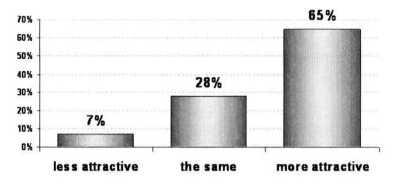

Figure 68: Ranking of all-in-one platform solutions over time.
(Purdue Research Foundation)

Given the complexity of running a contact center, anything that can be done to simplify it is appreciated by management. Both the sample statistics above and the site visits confirmed that there is a widely-held impression that companies offering all-in-one solutions have made positive strides in recent years to make their offerings more comprehensive and useful. Thus, the numbers show that a two thirds majority of respondents feel all-in-one platforms are rising in attractiveness, and only 7 % feel they are becoming less attractive.

What to Consider in an ROI Calculation

A Seven-Point ROI Methodology

When calculating ROI you will need a methodology. Table 8 is an example of ROI step-by-step methodology to use as a guideline. The steps in this process are: benchmark, segment, target, cost, predict, measure and continuous improvement. We have dedicated whole chapters to some of these topics, so they will not be covered here.

Table 8: Seven-point ROI Methodology (Purdue Research Foundation)

Step One - Benchmark
In this step, you get an objective measurement of the present operations and capture the key performance indicators.
Step Two - Segment
This step entails segmenting metrics into strategic categories, i.e., cost reduction, cost avoidance and/or revenue generation.
Step Three - Target
When targeting based on financial and strategic business objectives, you will want to prioritize select key metrics to focus on.
Step Four - Measure
Compare the metrics captured in the benchmarking stage with the results.
Step Five - Predict
Here, you forecast your breakeven point for the investment and estimate the total future gains.
Step Six - Cost and ROI
When measuring, you add the total cost of ownership for the implementation, including professional services, support, and training. This is where the ROI calculation is made.
Step Seven - Continuous Improvement
In this last step, you take the lessons learned and feed that back into the process to gain even more.

Step One – Benchmark: Benchmarking is covered in detail in chapter 9. For more information on benchmarking, we also suggest logging on to <www.BenchmarkPortal.com>. Here you will find white papers, how-to books, and other tools to help you benchmark your CRM center. Note that you will need to determine your key performance indicators (KPIs) in step one to be able to benchmark the "as is" conditions of your CRM center. We will explain more about KPIs later in this chapter.

Step Two – Segment: In this step you will want to segment the customers most important to you, and then determine the metrics that measure those particular customer segments based on your business goals, which can range from cost reduction to revenue generation.

Step Three – Target: We will use a CRM center as a concrete example to help you see, in this particular case, which KPIs show a direct correlation to customer satisfaction. By measuring the KPIs that have a direct correlation to customer satisfaction, you will be able to determine if you will hit your strategic goals. You will also be able to ascertain whether an ROI is possible. Later in the chapter we will provide case studies on ROI, but here we will go into some detail on KPIs. You can find more information by logging onto <www.BenchmarkPortal.com> and downloading a white paper called "Key Performance Indicators That Drive Customer Satisfaction."

In calculating an ROI for your own initiative, you will need to determine all your KPIs and then evaluate which are the best predictors of customer satisfaction in your company. This relates back to what we were talking about in chapter 5 when we discussed internal and external KPI's that are indicators of success. KPIs are internal metrics. So, in step three we would ask ourselves two questions:

- Which CRM center KPIs correlate best to customer satisfaction?
- What is the statistical relationship of each KPI to customer satisfaction?

Step Four – Measure: In the measure step, you would compare the metrics captured in the benchmarking stage with the results of the CRM improvement initiative after a specified amount of time. This means that you have established your KPIs before benchmarking and are using those same KPIs after the implementation to measure changes over time.

In order to translate the information from KPI measurements to ROI, one needs to look at the corresponding customer satisfaction improvements. The questions to ask yourself in this step are:

1. If the CRM center KPIs are improved, what is the corresponding customer satisfaction improvement that can be expected, if any?

2. When the CRM center KPIs are improved, what is the expected ROI, if any?

3. If call center KPIs are improved, what is the corresponding customer satisfaction improvement that can be expected, if any.

First, one looks at which KPIs are most relevant to what you are measuring. In this case, we are measuring the change in customer service. The three KPIs in table 8.5 were the only ones found to have a predictable relationship to incremental improvements in customer satisfaction. So these are the metrics that will be compared to determine the before-and-after results.

Table 9: Customer satisfaction Range (Purdue Research Foundation)

Customer Satisfaction Index Range									
Dissatisfied								Very Satisfied	
KPI	10%	20%	30%	40%	50%	60%	70%	80%	90%	100%
First/Final	58	59	68	64	69	68	76	74	73	74
Complaints	6	7	6	5	6	5	4	4	3	2
Abandon	7	7	9	6	6	5	5	5	5	5

<u>Step Five – Predict</u>: This step is where you look at the potential gains that can be made after the improvements are completed. Here you would forecast your breakeven point for the investment and estimate the total future gains.

Step Six – Cost and ROI: You will want to measure the total cost of ownership for the implementation including change management, profession services, support, and training. This is how much you are spending on the CRM technology implementation. The algorithms used to calculate the dollar value of changes in performance gaps are shown in table 8.6. The Purdue research team has developed a series of word formulas to calculate the cost savings and/or added customer lifetime value for improving all call center KPIs. You can begin to calculate the cost and resulting ROI for the improvement initiative for each KPI.

The formula for ROI is:

$$ROI = \frac{\textbf{Net Improvement Benefits}}{\textbf{Improvement Costs}}$$

$$ROI = \left(\frac{\textbf{Benefit of the Improvement – Cost of the Improvement}}{\textbf{Cost of the Improvement}} \right) \times 100$$

The benefit of the improvement is the total value of the change in performance gaps. The cost of the improvement is the total cost to implement the change for enhanced performance.

Step Seven – Continuous Improvement: You take the lessons learned and feed them back into the process to gain even more advantage by continuing to measure the most important KPIs. At this point you might also notice what else you might want to add to the system in your phased implementation for increased benefits.

REFERENCES

1. Anton J., Perkins, D., *Listening to the Voice of the Customer,* Customer Service Group

2. Anton, J., & Gustin, D ,*Call Center Benchmarking: How Good is Good Enough.* West Lafayette: Ichor Business Books.

3. Anton, J., *Call Center Management: By the Numbers.* West Lafayette: Ichor Business Books.

4. Anton, J., *The Voice of the Customer.* The Customer Service Group, New York, NY.

5. Anton, J., et al. *Customer Relationship Management.* Prentice-Hall, New York, NY.

6. Anton, J., & Johns, B. *Contact Center Best Practice Benchmarking.* Purdue University Center for Customer-Driven Quality, West Lafayette, IN.

7. Anton, J., "Is Your Contact Center an Asset or Liability?" *Support Solutions Magazine*, January.

8. Anton, J., "Quality of Service Standards." *Support Solutions Magazine*, May.

9. Anton, J., "Quality of Service Measurements." *Support Solutions Magazine*, June.

10. Anton, J., *Contact Center Best Practice Benchmarking.* Purdue University Center for Customer-Driven Quality, West Lafayette, IN.

11. Anton, J., *Corporate Mission Statements and Customer Satisfaction.* Purdue University Center for Customer-Driven Quality, West Lafayette, IN.

12. Anton, J., et al. *Call Center Design and Implementation.* Dame Publications, Houston, TX.

13. Bell, R., *Customers as Partners: Building Relationships that Last.* Kohler Publishers, Inc.

14. Rust, R., et al. *Return on Quality.* Probus Publishing, Chicago, IL.

15. Reichfield, F.F., "Loyalty-Based Management." *The Harvard Business Review.*

16. Anton, J., & de Ruyter, J.C.,"Van Klachten naar Managementinformatie." *Harvard Holland Business Review,* p27.

17. Bitner, M.J., et al "The Service Encounter." *The Journal of Marketing.*

18. Burgers, A., & Anton J. *The Impact of Image on Revenue.* Purdue University Center for Customer-Driven Quality, West Lafayette, IN.

19. *Call Center Excellence: Continuous Improvement Boosts Performance*; PR Newswire, New York, NY; Nov 14, 2001. Retrieved December 13, 2001 from the ProQuest Direct database on the World Wide Web: http://www.proquest.umi.com/

20. Vish Thirumurthy, Group Product Manager for the Customer Care Framework Product at Microsoft.

21. Terri Zwierzynski @.Solo-E.com

22. Liz Roche, Managing Partner, Customers Incorporated.

23. Robert Bascal, *Perfect Phrases for Performance For Customer Service*

24. Robert Bascal, *Defusing Hostile Customers Workbook*

25. SCORE, *Counselors to America's Small Business*

26. Jill Griffen, President-Griffen Group

27. Bill Owen, Schedule planning Lead Planner, Southwest Airlines

28. U.S. Department of Commerce

29. Claud Borna, *Telecommunications Magazine*

30. Terry G. Vavra, Improving Your Measurement of Customer Satisfaction: A Guide to Creating, Conducting, Analyzing, and Reporting Customer Satisfaction Measurement Programs

31. *SMART Customer Satisfaction Measurement*, SMART.com

32. Dick Bucci, *Post-Call Customer Satisfaction Measurement*

33. Derek R. Allen, Tanniru R. Rao, *Analysis of Customer Satisfaction Data*

34. Bob E. Hayes, *Measuring Customer Satisfaction Data*

35. Nigel Hill, Jim Alexander, *Handbook of Customer Satisfaction and Loyalty*

36. Nikolaos F. Matsatsinis, E. Ioannidou, E. Grigoroudis, *Customer Satisfaction Using Data Mining Techniques*

37. The Resource Center for Customer Service Professionals, *Customer Satisfaction and Loyalty Data: Analysis and Interpretation*

38. Hernon, Peter, John R. Whitman, *Delivering Satisfaction and Service Quality*

39. Bob Hayes, *Measuring **Customer Satisfaction**: **Survey** Design, Use, and Statistical **Analysis** Methods*

40. Robert B. Woodruff, Sarah Gardial, *Know Your Customer; New Approaches to Understanding Customer Value and Satisfaction*

41. Web Fletcher, *Satisfaction: Guaranteed?*

42. KNOVA Software, *White Paper: Increase Customer Satisfaction by Understanding the Intelligent Customer Lifecycle*

43. Kevin Cacioppo, *Measuring and Managing Customer Satisfaction*

44. David L. Kurtz, Louis E. Boone, *Contemporary Marketing*

Author Biographies

Co-Author

 **Dr. Jon Anton** (also known as "Dr. Jon") is an Adjunct Professor at Purdue University and the Director of Benchmark Research at Center for Customer-Driven Quality™ at Purdue. He specializes in enhancing customer service strategy through inbound call centers, and e-business centers, using the latest in telecommunications (voice), and computer (digital) technology. He also focuses on using the Internet for external customer access, as well as Intranets and middleware.

Since 1995, Dr. Jon has been the principal investigator of the Purdue University Call Center Benchmark Research. This data is now collected at the BenchmarkPortal.com Web site, where it is placed into a data warehouse that currently contains over ten million data points on call center performance.

Dr. Jon has assisted over 400 companies in improving their customer service strategy/delivery by the design and implementation of inbound and outbound call centers, as well as in the decision-making process of using teleservices providers for maximizing service levels while minimizing costs per call. In August of 1996, *Call Center Magazine* honored Dr. Jon by selecting him as an Original Pioneer of the emerging call center industry. In October of 2000, Dr. Jon was named to the Call Center Hall of Fame. In January of 2001, Dr. Jon was selected for the industry's "Leaders and Legends" Award by

Help Desk 2000. Dr. Jon is also a member of the National Committee for Quality Assurance.

Dr. Jon has guided corporate executives in strategically re-positioning their call centers as robust customer access centers through a combination of benchmarking, re-engineering, consolidation, outsourcing, and Web-enablement. The resulting single point of contact for the customer allows business to be conducted anywhere, anytime, and in any form. By better understanding the customer lifetime value, Dr. Jon has developed techniques for calculating the ROI for customer service initiatives.

Dr. Jon has published 117 papers on customer service and call center methods in industry journals. In 1997, one of his papers on self-service was awarded the best article of the year by *Customer Relationship Management Magazine*.

Dr. Jon has published twenty-four professional books:

1. *Enabling IVR Self-Service with Speech Recognition*

2. *Contact Center Management By The Numbers*

3. *Managing Web-Based Customer Experiences*

4. *From Cost to Profit Center: How Technology Enables the Difference*

5. *Customer Service and the Human Experience: We, the People, Make a Difference*

6. *Customer Service at a Crossroads*

7. *Offshore Outsourcing Opportunities*

8. *Optimizing Outbound Calling*

9. *Customer Relationship Management Technology*

10. *Customer Obsession: Your Roadmap to Profitable CRM*

11. *Integrating People with Process and Technology*

12. *Selecting a Teleservices Partner*

13. *How to Conduct a Call Center Performance Audit: A to Z*

14. *20:20 CRM A Visionary Insight into Unique Customer Contact*

15. *Minimizing Agent Turnover*

16. *e-Business Customer Service*

17. *Customer Relationship Management*

18. *Call Center Performance Enhancement Using Simulation and Modeling*

19. *Call Center Benchmarking: How Good is "Good Enough"*

20. *Listening to the Voice of the Customer*

21. *Contact Center Management by the Numbers*

22. *Customer Relationship Management: Making Hard Decisions with Soft Numbers*

23. *Inbound Customer Contact Center Design*

24. *Computer-Assisted Learning*

25. *Experience Customer Care: "Going Beyond Customer Service"*

26. *Interpreting the Voice of the Customer*

Dr. Jon's formal education was in technology, including a Doctorate of Science and a Master of Science from Harvard University, a Master of Science from the University of Connecticut, and a Bachelor of Science from the University of Notre Dame. He also completed a three-summer intensive Executive Education program in Business at the Graduate School of Business at Stanford University.

Dr. Jon can be reached at Purdue University at 765-494-8357 or at BenchmarkPortal at <DrJonAnton@BenchmarkPortal.com.

Co-Author

 **Kevin L. Childs,** EVP and President of Sales, Marketing and Support- Mr. Childs joined UCN in 2002 at the inception of the company's on-demand, contact center application initiative to create a complete contact routing and agent management solution. He played a key role in the acquisition of the technologies at the core of UCN's flagship product, inContactR and led the execution of UCN's Software-as-a-Service business strategy. Mr. Childs co-authored the book, "Interpreting the Voice of the Customer".

Prior to UCN, he held a number of senior leadership positions with Adecco, a Swiss-based, human capital company. While at Adecco, he led a $100m operation, a staff of 120 and 4,500 associates, supporting human capital initiatives for Florida-based employers and many contact centers for leading US-based financial institutions and Fortune 1000. His clients included BofA, CitiBank, JP MorganChase, Verizon, and MetLife.

He also spent eight years at the Salt Lake City-based operation of SOS Services, where again he was involved in contact center projects.

Mr. Childs holds a B.S. in business management from University of Phoenix.

Content Editor

John Chatterley is a Senior Content Editor specializing contact center performance research, analysis, technical writing, and content editing. John has published numerous customized benchmarking reports, research reports, One-Minute Survey reports, and White Papers. Mr. Chatterley co-authored books entitled "Offshore Outsourcing Opportunities," "Selecting a Teleservices Partner," and "Automated Self-Service Using Speech Recognition," Experience Customer Care …Going Beyond Customer Service," "Interpreting the Voice of the Customer," and is currently working on several others.

Mr. Chatterley is also analyst/writer/editor of BenchmarkPortal's annual series of 42 detailed industry reports covering the spectrum of contact center industry sectors. He authored a comprehensive White Paper study entitled "Improving Contact Center Performance through Optimized Site Selection."

John's professional career spans more than 20 years of experience in call center management and consulting. Mr. Chatterley designed, implemented, staffed and managed three 500+ seat contact center sites in Arizona, Nevada, and California, and has extensive call center operational management experience. He possesses first-hand experience at all levels of a contact center including front-line technical support agent, supervisor, team lead, analyst, designer, call center manager, and operations director.

John is a Purdue Certified Contact Center Auditor, Certified AT&T Call Center College Instructor, BenchmarkPortal Certified Benchmarking Instructor and Analyst. John's professional education was in Electrical Engineering & Computer Science at Southern Utah University, and subsequently at the University of Utah.

APPENDIX A: CASE STUDIES

Two Customer Feedback Case Studies

Case Study #1

In the late 1990s, while the diagnostic imaging market was expanding at a clip of about 10% each year, growth at Toshiba America Medical Systems Inc. (Tustin, CA) was stagnant. The company was losing customers as fast as it was adding them. To understand the reasons why, the company's leaders implemented a new formal research process—and were horrified to learn the results. Customers were not at all happy with the company's performance.

For Toshiba, the key lesson that emerged during the research process was that what customers value seemed to be different from what the company and its employees believed they value. Toshiba determined that the benchmarks the company had used to establish success were not the benchmarks that customers most appreciated. As a result, customer dissatisfaction permeated all areas of the company's performance.

Following these discoveries, Toshiba's executive team began developing a philosophy and programs to support the company's drive to develop and maintain long-term customer-focused relationships. The company consolidated its research activities and launched a new centralized, formal survey and response process.

Then Toshiba faced an even more significant challenge: the cultural change required for success. Much of the company's work force found it difficult to embrace the idea of ongoing solicitation of customer feedback as a positive step toward companywide improvement. At first, the honest feedback seemed to spawn only finger-pointing and blame for things gone wrong. In fact, company executives estimate that it took nearly two years of focused effort to reshape Toshiba's corporate culture into one that accepts missteps as opportunities for improvement.

The cultural transition gradually took root, and Toshiba began to see increased market share. Since that time, the company has more than doubled its annual sales to about $700 million. Today the company is ranked number one in many of the product categories in which it competes, and its efforts to reform its corporate culture have catapulted Toshiba from last in the imaging sector to first, in both growth and user satisfaction ratings.

Case Study #2

Southwest Airlines recently introduced DING!, a free program that sends audible electronic notices to a consumer's desktop. Today's dinged fares typically undercut Southwest's published fares. But industry analysts and other carriers looking into similar services say some, especially those hitting satisfied business travelers, will raise prices based on the convenience and timely consideration (something road warriors will appreciate) of the delivery.

Custom fares fill unsold seats efficiently and groom customer segments to their revenue potential.

Until DING!, carriers have used modeling techniques to predict demand, then released unsold tickets to third-party sellers that collected a fee for every transaction. Southwest (and competitors that surely will follow it) keeps communication direct between the carrier and the customer. It also pulls in personal information about passengers. With this information the airlines can build better predictive models for ticket sales as well as understand what extra value to bundle with their services in order to maximize profit margin among extremely satisfied customers.

Two Statistical Analysis Case Studies

Case Study #3

This is an actual example, witnessed by the authors in a banking customer service call center.

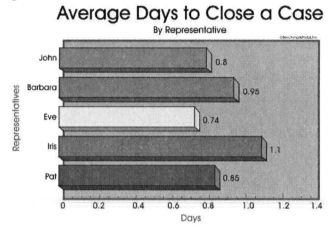

Figure 69: Average days to close – by agent. (Purdue Research Foundation)

From this figure, the supervisor might conclude that all the agents are reasonably equal in their ability to close cases.

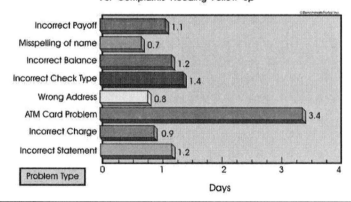

Figure 70: Average days to close – for complaints needing follow-up. (Purdue Research Foundation)

By drilling down on the problems causing complaints, the supervisor can see that ATM card problems are by far the most common issue that needs to be addressed based purely on the time these take to resolve.

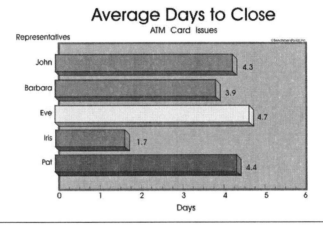

Figure 71: Average days to close – by ATM issue. (Purdue Research Foundation)

If the supervisor re-cuts the data based on the agent's ability to close the ATM card problems, an opportunity seems to surface, and that is that Iris seem to close these cases much quicker than others.

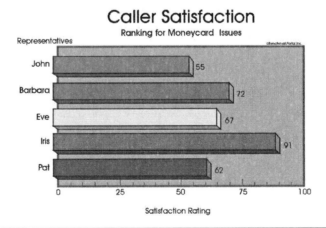

Figure 72: Average days to close – ranking for money card issues. (Purdue Research Foundation)

139

Just to ensure that Iris is not just "faster" but maybe there is a quality issue, the supervisors does a quick drill-down on customer satisfaction with this type of call. In this report, it becomes obvious that Iris is not only faster in solving the "ATM money card issue" but that she gets the highest customer satisfaction scores as well. So the obvious action to take by the supervisor is to learn from Iris specifically how she solves the ATM money card issue for callers.

Case Study #4

This is an actual example, witness by the authors in an airline customer service call center.

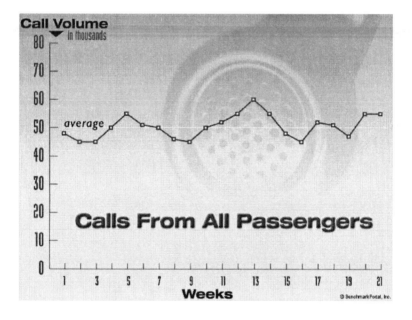

Figure 73: Inbound call volume over time (period one).

140

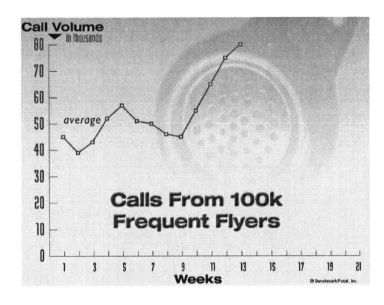

Figure 74: Inbound call volume over time.

After a reasonable level call volume over time graph, suddenly the call volume begins to increase alarmingly over a period of four weeks, cause staffing issues.

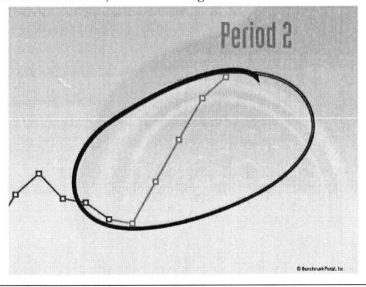

Figure 75: Inbound call volume over time (period two).

The challenge then becomes to study Period Two to determine what is driving this increased call volume.

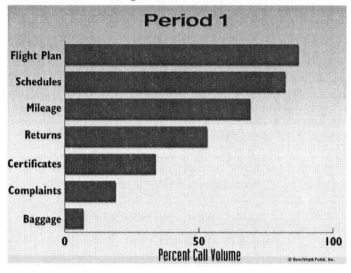

Figure 76: Period one call type frequencies.

If we study the call types during period one, this figure shows the frequency distribution. Notice that complaints are number two from the bottom, i.e. not a big issue.

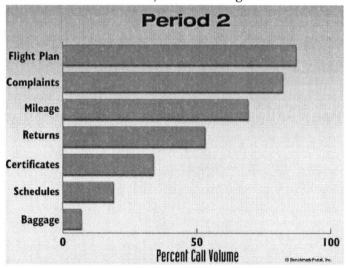

Figure 77: Period two call type frequencies.

If we study the call types during period two, this figure shows the frequency distribution. Notice that complaints are now number two from the top, i.e. a big issue.

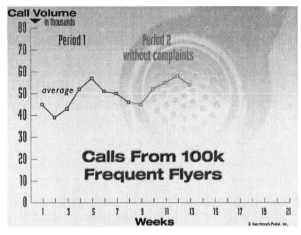

Figure 78: Call volume in period two plotted without complaints.

Notice that if we remove the added complaint volume, the call volume graphs becomes normal again, indicating that the primary issue is a large increase in passengers calling to complain.

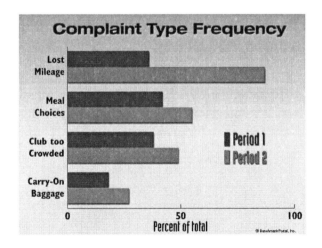

Figure 79: Complaint type frequencies.

143

If we then plot the complaint type frequencies for period one versus two, it becomes immediately clear that passengers are calling to complain about a change in their "earned mileage" program. This was a time when this airline announced that if earned mileage was not used by the end of the year the frequent flyer would lose the mileage.

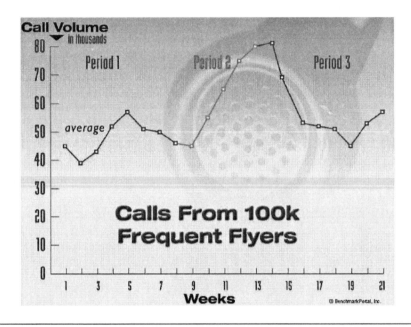

Figure 80: Call volume in period three

When the airline in question, reversed their policy related to using earned mileage, the complaints decreased, and the call volume returned back to normal.

144

Case Study – Audience Satisfaction Survey

Here is an example of an audience satisfaction survey taken after a keynote presentation that was delivered to the conference attendees at the annual 2007 Call Center Campus, sponsored by Purdue University in Lafayette, Illinois:

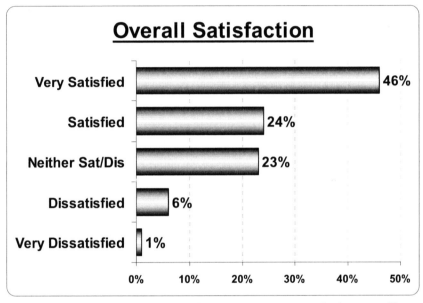

This chart depicts the audience response to their overall satisfaction with the keynote presentation

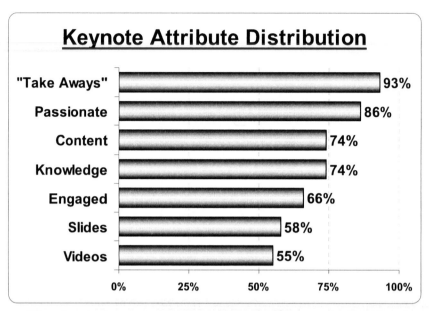

The chart above ranks the audience response to the listed attributes of the keynote address.

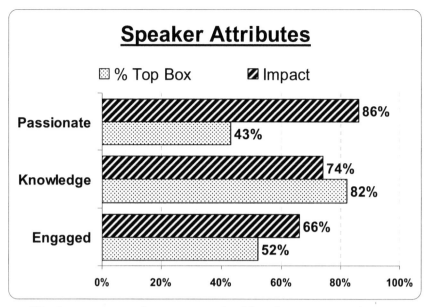

The keynote speaker was ranked by the presentation impact alongside the percentage of the audience that awarded a perfect 5 out of 5 "Top Box" score to the speaker.

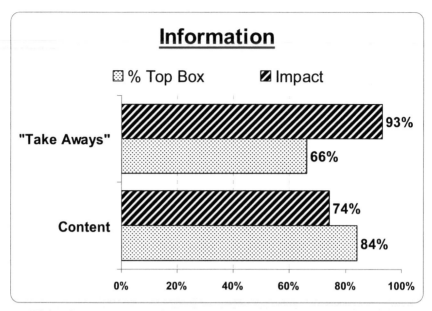

This chart compared % Top Box scores with the impact of the information content of the presentation.

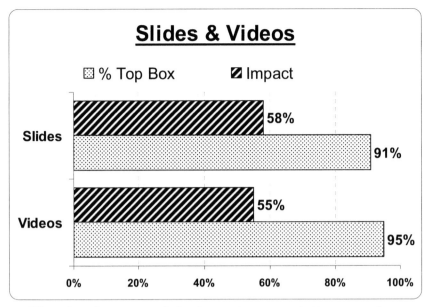

The visual content of the keynote presentation was also ranked by the audience for % Top Box perfect scores and visual impact.

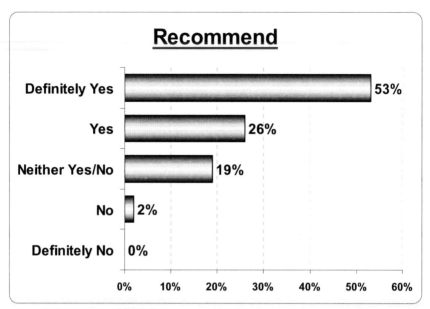

Finally, the audience of the keynote presentation was asked to indicate their willingness to recommend the speaker to a colleague or friend.

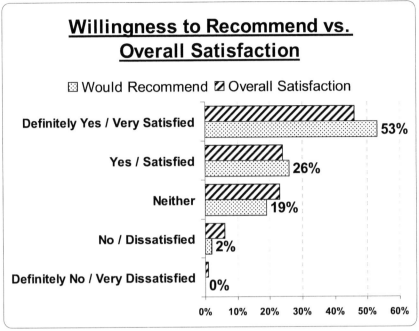

This chart compares the audiences' willingness to recommend with their overall satisfaction of the presentation. This comparison is a useful "sanity check" to validate the audience responses to this survey. As you can see, their responses to overall satisfaction track fairly closely to their overall satisfaction ranking, and thus validates the survey.

Appendix B: Customer Satisfaction Survey Examples

Customer Satisfaction Survey Example

The following is a call center survey that has been used to successfully measure external customer satisfaction metrics using an automated voice-response (VRU) computer assisted survey process. You will find much more information about the survey process in Appendix E. The user of this handbook can modify this survey to better-fit specific call center needs while maintaining the structure and function of the original survey.

"Hello, and welcome to _____'s survey. We want to continue to make telephone service improvements based on the feedback we gather from callers like you. We appreciate your willingness to share your opinion of the telephone service you just received."

1. _____ Would you say your question was answered or your problem resolved as a result of this call? Respond by saying "yes" or "no."

For the next several questions, please grade our telephone agent on a 1 to 5 scale with 5 being "the best" and 1 being "the worst."

2. _____ Quickly understood your request.

3. _____ Showed concern when answering your question.

4. _____ Spoke clearly.

5. _____ Had sufficient knowledge about our products and services.

6. _____ Gave a complete answer.

7. _____ Gave you confidence in the solution or answer.

8. _____ Clearly presented your options.

9. _____ Completed your call as quickly as possible.

10. _____ All things considered, on the 1 to 10 scale with 10 being high, how satisfied were you with this call?

11. _____ Because of this interaction with our telephone agent, how likely are you to continue your service?

12. _____ In the future, how likely are you to recommend our company to a friend?

13. What is one thing that we could have done better in handling your call..

Thank you very much for your time. Your opinions will be helpful in providing the best possible service to you in the future.

E-mail Satisfaction Survey Example

The following is a contact center e-mail survey that has been used to successfully measure external customer satisfaction metrics using an automated e-mail response computer assisted process. You will find much more information about the survey process in Appendix B. The user of this handbook can modify this survey to better-fit specific call center needs while maintaining the structure and function of the original survey.

"Hello, and welcome to _____'s survey. We want to continue to make telephone service improvements based on the feedback we gather from callers like you. We appreciate your willingness to share your opinion of the telephone service you just received."

1. _____ Would you say your question was answered or your problem resolved as a result of this call? Respond by typing "yes" or "no."

For the next several questions, please grade our e-mail agent on a 1 to 5 scale with 5 being "the best" and 1 being "the worst."

2. _____ Completely understood your request.

3. _____ Displayed concern when answering your question.

4. _____ Explained himself/herself clearly.

5. _____ Had sufficient knowledge about our products and services.

6. _____ Provided a complete answer.

7. _____ Gave you confidence in the solution or answer.

8. _____ Clearly presented your options.
9. _____ Responded to your e-mail promptly.
10. _____ All things considered, on the 1 to 10 scale with 10 being high, how satisfied were you with this e-mail contact?
11. _____ Because of this interaction with our e-mail agent, how likely are you to continue your service?
12. _____ In the future, how likely are you to recommend our company to a friend?

Thank you very much for your time. Your opinions will be helpful in providing the best possible service to you in the future.

Appendix C: Sampling Concepts

A basic determinant of survey research quality is the proper utilization of a random sample of customers. Random samples permit the use of various statistical techniques to describe and predict the behavior of all customers. The idea is simple: if you draw at random enough times, eventually you will draw a sample that is representative (i.e., reflective) of the population from which the sample is drawn.

The second determinant of the quality of a data-gathering program is whether or not it allows you to contact a representative sample of your customers. A useful example can be found in the survey research conducted by large polling firms to provide information about political choices, attitudes about controversial topics, and other data relevant to current affairs. These surveys typically range in size from 500 to 1,500 respondents and are usually representative samples of the American public. It is because they are representative samples that the results can be used to say something with 95% confidence about the opinions and behaviors of all adult Americans.

These professional pollsters have some assurance that the sample is representative because it was randomly drawn from the population of interest and is quite large. Probability theory assures us that under these circumstances we will have attained representativeness (within known probabilities) because the characteristics of the sample approximate the characteristics of the population.

Contact center managers should have the same goal for their caller CS measurement programs. The concept of representativeness simply means that along the pre-defined characteristics, the random sample mirrors the characteristics of the population of callers to which you wish to generalize your survey research results. To determine necessary sample sizes refer to Figure 71.

Margin of Error

Confidence	10%	5%	3%	2%	1%
80%	41	164	455	1,024	4,096
90%	68	272	756	1,702	6,806
95%	96	384	1,067	2,401	9,604
98%	136	543	1,508	3,393	13,572
99%	166	666	1,849	4,160	16,641

Figure 81. Sampling proportions for large populations

Most companies will have sub-populations within the population of all customers. These segments are more typically called segments and refer to such divergent customer groupings as end-user consumers versus business-to-business customers. Important groups within those sub-populations may also exist. The sampling frame for future phases of the CS program must address these sub-populations by using a stratified random sample.

To illustrate, imagine a computer mail-order house with the customer base segmented into three groups: household, business, and government users. We would want the sample to be drawn from those three segments in proportion to their size since it is likely that each of these three groups has very different customer needs. When this is accomplished, we say that our sample is representative (at least with respect to the limited set of criteria used to segment the customers). It is imperative to collect enough data to satisfy statistical confidence limits. Your measurement program must yield results that are statistically representative of the callers within each group.

APPENDIX D: EXTERNAL METRIC ANALYSIS

This appendix contains important information on how to analyze the external data you have so carefully gathered. The analysis described in this part can be applied to the customer satisfaction survey instrument in Appendix A. Several analytical concepts are presented to enhance the value of the information generated from the data. CS data must be available for analysis in a timely manner. The obvious goal of collecting customer opinions of your service is to make changes to your processes that will increase customer satisfaction. Such changes need to be made quickly in response to market pressures and to avoid further market damage that is caused by a poor service attribute.

Risk Analysis

Another helpful analytic tool is a technique called risk analysis. The theory behind this technique is that the original variables are recoded into just two groups: those with low ratings and those with high ratings. The definition of high and low will vary depending on the number of scale points. Each service attribute variable for which this analysis can be completed does not have to be collapsed to the same scale. Once this grouping is done, the upper left cell are those customers who gave both low ratings to overall satisfaction (or likelihood to continue service) and a specific attribute.

Overall Satisfaction

	1 - 4	5 - 7
Individual 1 - 4	**15%**	**15%**
Attributes 5 - 7	**10%**	**60%**

Figure 82. Example recoding for vulnerability analysis

With this information in Figure 82, you can suggest the following:

1. It was this low attribute rating which contributed to 15% of customers having lower overall satisfaction ratings. Further analysis can identify these customers and a root cause analysis can determine why they rated this service attribute low.

2. The 15% of customers in the upper right cell place little importance on the specific attribute when assigning an overall satisfaction score.

3. The 10% of customers in the lower left cell must rate other attributes poorly to cause the lower overall satisfaction rating.

Vulnerability tables can be generated for any number of measured attributes and a comparison of the percentages in the upper left cell across tables can identify where your risk is greater; i.e., where more customers rate an attribute and overall satisfaction lower.

The technique is called risk analysis because of the assumption that the customers located in the upper left cell are at risk of discontinuing service and that this risk is caused, at least in part, by this specific service attribute. Note that we said in part. Many forces determine customer attitudes, so great reliance should never be placed on a single bivariate analysis except in unusual circumstances such as when performance is so poor (or wonderful) that it dominates all other attributes.

An example of risk analysis is displayed in Figure 83. Only 5.6% of the customers appear to be at risk with the vast majority rating both variables at high levels. It is important to realize that the large number of customers in the bottom right cell can also mean that overall quality ratings help cause overall satisfaction. These customers are not at risk and there is no immediate danger of losing them, but we need to keep quality high so that they remain customers. Conversely, there is immediate cause for concern for the 5.6% in the low satisfaction condition.

Overall Satisfaction

Satisfaction with Overall Quality	Lower Overall Satisfaction		Higher Overall Satisfaction	
Lower Satisfaction	28	5.60%	50	18.10%
Higher Satisfaction	56	11.90%	362	17.00%

Figure 83. An example of risk analysis

APPENDIX E: INTERNAL AND EXTERNAL SURVEY

Scripting, Questions, and Identification of Internal Metrics

Note: Script to be heard by customer appears in quotations.

"Hello, and welcome to _____ 's automated survey. We continue to make service improvements based on the feedback we gather from callers like you. We appreciate your willingness to share your opinion of the service you just received when calling us."

"Please use any number from 1 to 5 to grade the following with 5 being 'most acceptable' and 1 being 'least acceptable.'"

Internal Metric to Be Captured per Call	Customer Perception
# of rings	"The # of rings you heard before the menu choices were presented."
Queue time—ACD answers	"The length of time you spent on hold waiting for the first telephone until advocate answers agent to answer."
Hold time	"During the call, the length of time placed on hold by the telephone agent. If your call was not placed on hold, press 0."
# of transfers	"The need for one agent to transfer you to a different agent to complete your call. If you were not transferred, press 0."

"For the following characteristics, grade the agent using the 1 to 5 scale with 5 being the highest score and 1 being the lowest."

Internal Metric to Be Captured per Call	Customer Perception
# of transfers	"Agent's knowledge of the company's products and services."
Talk time	"Agent spent enough time with you in handling your call."

"Again, with 5 being the highest and 1 being the lowest, rate the following:"

"How satisfied were you with the overall service you received on this call?"

"As a result of this call, how likely are you to continue your service with our company?"

Internal Metric to Be Be Captured per Call	Customer Perception
'First call resolution'	"Did the advocate answer your question or solve your problem during this call? Answer yes or no."

"Thank you very much for your time. Your opinions will be very useful for us in planning the best possible service for you in the future. Good bye."

Additional metrics to be captured from ACD data, or calculated from ACD data concurrent to the call:

- blocked call % at time of call
- abandonment rate at time of call
- time to abandonment at time of call
- after call work time average at time of call
- status of agent (i.e., full-time or part-time and tenure in months)

APPENDIX F: DATA TYPES IN SURVEY DESIGN

Nominative Data

Definition: This is typical the data with which we identify the survey respondent.

Examples: Simple examples of nominative data would include the respondent's name, name of the company for whom the respondent, what is the birth city of the respondent, and the like.

Potential Scales: Nominative data cannot be scaled. Nominative data must be the absolute value of the data sought.

Statistical Analysis: Nominative data that is unique to the respondent cannot be used in statistical analysis. However, nominative data that is not unique to any individual respondent, like city of birth, can be used to group data on which various statistical analysis can be performed. For instance, if we group all respondents living in the State of California, we can study these respondents as compared to respondents in other States in the Union.

Relative Value: Nominative data is extremely valuable in survey analysis as it allows us to compare groups of respondents with the same nominative data. This "cut" of the survey database can yield statistically significant differences between respondents in different groupings.

Numerical Data

Definition: Numerical data are simply just that...numbers.

Examples: Where possible ask the respondent for actual numerical data, for instance, how old are you in years? Other examples might be zip code (only in the US are they numeric), or number of agents, and the like.

Potential Scales: Numerical data can be scaled by grouping potential numerical answers for the respondent. For instance, how many agents work at your call center? Less than 20, from 20 to 50, from 51 to 100, over 100.

Statistical Analysis: Numerical data are perfect for almost all statistical analysis routines, i.e., averages, means, variances, standard deviations, and significance tests. Where possible, don't use scales or give ranges for the respondent to select from. Scales and ranges greatly dilute the power of analyzing numerical data. Scales and ranges literally "dumb down" useful numerical data.

Relative Value: Numerical data are very valuable in determining statistically significant customer feedback.

Alpha-Numerical Data

Definition: Alpha-numerical data are simply just that…a combination of letters and numbers.

Examples: Where possible ask the respondent for the actual alpha-numeric data, for instance what is the number on your driver's license? (often alpha-numeric)

Potential Scales: Alpha-numeric data cannot easily be scaled.

Statistical Analysis: Alpha-numeric data are not easily used in statistical analysis. Like nominal data, alpha-numeric data is best used to group respondents for further statistical comparisons.

Relative Value: Alpha-numerical data are not very valuable in customer survey feedback analysis.

Dichotomous Data

Definition: Dichotomous data are those data points that have only two states.

Examples: An example of dichotomous data would be "was your problem resolved on the call"….yes or no. Therefore, only two values are possible, and the respondent must pick one of them.

Potential Scales: Dichotomous data are only used in the scaled approach, for instance, a) yes or no, b) one or zero, and c) stop or start.

Statistical Analysis: Dichotomous data are very easily analyzed statistically and lend themselves to highly accurate feedback from the customer.

Relative Value: Dichotomous data are very valuable for customer feedback analysis.

Categorical Data

Definition: Categorical data are descriptive in nature, and often have the effect of dividing respondents into various categories.

Examples: An example of categorical data is the question "what industry is your company in? This might have answers like Financial Services, Health Maintenance, and the like.

Potential Scales: Categorical data cannot be scaled, however, the respondent can be given numerous realistic choices, and then an "other" category in case the suggested choices do not fit.

Statistical Analysis: Categorical data does not lend itself to statistical analysis. Like nominal data, categorical data can be used to group respondents and then do statistical analysis on the differences between groupings. For instance, how did the Financial Services respondents differ from the Travel/Leisure industry respondents?

Relative Value: Categorical data has definite value in comparing populations of respondents. One can also combine categorical and nominative data by for instance, running a statistical comparison tab on all Financial Services respondents located in the State of California.

Multiple-Choice Data

Definition: Often there are one or more answers to a survey question posed to a customer respondent. Multiple-choice data are those data points that can be selected by respondent to give the most likely answer.

Examples: A survey may query the respondent as follows: "Which of the following best describes your emotional state when the product arrived broken?" A series of anticipated plausible answers would be provided.

Potential Scales: Multi-choice data cannot be scaled since each answer must be realistic to the respondent. In fact, multiple-choice data often include the suggestion to the respondent: "please check all that apply."

Statistical Analysis: Multi-choice data lends itself primarily to doing frequency tables of how often any one choice was selected by the respondent. Multi-choice data also lends itself well to regression analysis.

Relative Value: Multiple-choice data is very valuable in analyzing customer feedback and producing actionable reports.

Qualitative Data

Definition: Qualitative data are those data points where the respondent is asked to give a qualitative opinion about a company's product and/or service.

Examples: An example of qualitative data is the answer to the question "Overall how satisfied were you with how we managed your telephone experience?" Various choices of answers would follow.

Potential Scales: Scales are always a source of controversy, yet in our experience, there is truly only one logical choice for American respondents. For statistical analysis, scales must have a neutral point to be effective. Choices for scales include:

1. Ask the respondent to select 1, 2, or 3, where 1 = poor, 2 = neutral, and 3 = excellent. What's good about this scale is that it is simple. What's not good about this scale is that it is not granular enough.

2. Ask the respondent to select 1, 2, 3, 4, or 5, where 1 = very dissatisfied, 2 = dissatisfied, 3 = neither satisfied or dissatisfied, 4 = satisfied, and 5 = very satisfied. What's good about this scale is that Americans are accustomed to qualitative 5-point scales....witness the most popular grading of system in schools is A, B, C, D, or F. We can easily understand the difference between an A and a B, or a D versus an F. And we know that C is neither good nor bad.

3. Ask the respondent to select 1, 2, 3, 4, 5, 6, or 7, again where there is some sliding definition for each number. What is not good about this scale is that most Americans cannot understand

the difference between a 5 versus a 6, or a 2 versus a 3. This will result in varying degrees of understanding by the respondent, and much greater variances in the results.

4. For scales that go from 1 to 10, there is no mid-point and also there are just too many choices. The respondents get confused, and the variance in the data is such that analyst begin combining numbers, like grouping all 9s and 10s, 6s and 7s, and before you know it you're back to a five-point scale. Scales of from 1 to 10 are not a good approach statistically.

Statistical Analysis: The five point scale lends itself very well to statistical analysis since it includes a neutral point from which the trend can be documented and tested statistically.

Relative Value: Qualitative data is very important in customer feedback in that it allows us to quantify the qualitative opinions and emotions of customers.

Textual Data

Definition: In seeking customer feedback through a survey, it is good design to at some point ask the customer an open-ended question. The answer to such an open-ended question is referred to as textual data.

Examples: An example of textual data could be as follows: "Regarding your call experience, what is one thing we could have done better?" A verbatim window appears, and the customer is asked to articulate their answer and/or suggestion.

Potential Scales: Textual data cannot be scaled.

Statistical Analysis: Textual data cannot be analyzed statistically unless it is converted to numerical data.

Relative Value: Textual data can be very valuable, however the analysis of textual data is tedious and very time consuming. It is however, truly the "voice of the customer," and therefore should not be overlooked in survey data analysis.

Appendix G: Important Statistical Concepts

Simple Regression

The point was made earlier that the customer perception of the operational dimensions of the contact center should be used when setting the service level goals for your contact center. Several types of analyses can provide you with strong, quantitative tools to set these service level goals.

We propose the use of simple linear regression models. Regression is a technique to predict the value of a dependent variable (usually called "y") as follows:

$$y = B0 + B1X + e$$

Where **y** = dependent variable. In the case of a contact center CS survey, this is the caller's perception of the internal metric as seen in the table in Appendix E.

X = independent variable or predictor of y. In the case of a contact center CS survey, these are all the metrics as captured from the ACD at the same time that the caller was on the phone plus any pertinent data from Accounting or Human Resources.

e = random error, it is usually assumed to be 0

B0 = y-intercept of the line through the y-axis

B1 = slope of the line, amount of increase or decrease in y for every 1 unit increase or decrease in **X**.

Repeating from above, the independent variable or X would be the per call actual metrics as captured from the ACD. The dependent variable, or y, is the customer's perception of the metric as rated during the CS survey.

The regression technique plots each X and y pair of values on a coordinate axis. See Figure 84 for a plot of data points. In this case, the vertical axis provides the level of the dependent variable (satisfaction with the call) and the horizontal axis the level of the independent variable (actual talk time). The following graphs use a scale from 1 to 5.

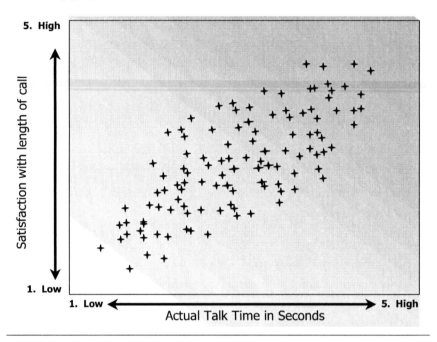

Figure 84. Plot of independent and dependent variable pairs

The intersection of those two levels is the location of that data pair, represented by points on the scatter plot shown in Figure 84. For example, on a set of coordinate axes, one axis would indicate the number of minutes of talk time that actually occurred with caller #1 as reported by the ACD (say 3 minutes), and the other axis would indicate caller #1's perception of satisfaction on "spent enough time with you in handling your call" (say very satisfied, or a 5). The intersection of these two levels (3, 5) would be the location of that pair of values. All data pairs are plotted, and then the regression algorithm places a line of best fit through the data. In Figure 85, we have added the regression line by using simple statistics. The line is defined by the equation:

$$y = B0 + B1X, \text{ as explained in Appendix E.}$$

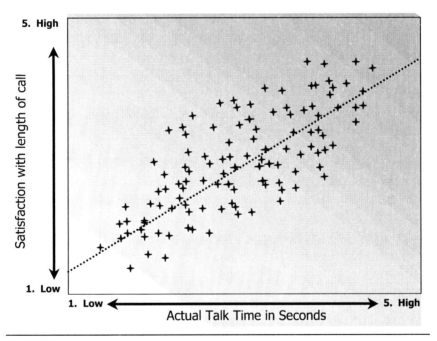

Figure 85. Example of a regression line

Three relationships may exist between the X and y variables. The relationship may be negative (downward sloping with respect to the point of origin) which means that as the independent variable (X) decreases, the dependent variable (y) increases. In this case, B1 (widely known as Beta) is a negative number, so the slope of the line is negative. One would expect a negative relationship in situation where a metric such as "queue time" is too long. An improvement opportunity exists in this case because the satisfaction with "queue time" (y) decreases as actual length of queue time (X) increases.

The relationship may be positive (the line slopes upward with respect to the point of origin) which means that as the independent variable (X) increases the dependent variable (y) increases. In this case, B1 (Beta) is a positive number, which means the slope of the line is upward. One would expect a positive relationship to exist between "satisfaction with spending enough time with the customer" (y) and "talk time" (X). If agents were hurrying to increase their number of calls handled and, therefore, rushing callers off the phone, 'talk time' will decrease, but "satisfaction" will also decrease.

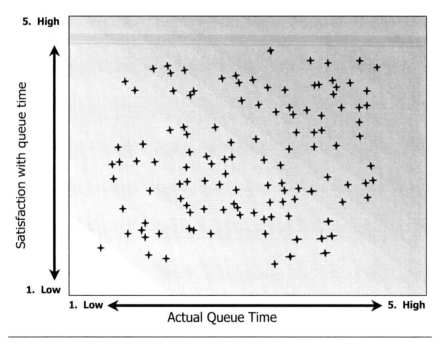

Figure 86. Two variables that are not related

If the two variables were completely unrelated, the true slope of the line (B1) would be zero, which means that X contributes no information for the prediction of y. In this situation, the manager can infer that focusing on that metric will not generate a change in satisfaction. An example of this can be seen in Figure 86.

Case Study One

Situation

This case study is based on a situation comparing "time in the queue" as the independent variable (X) and "satisfaction with queue time" as the dependent variable (y). Using the regression results to substitute into the equation, an example for the variable "time in queue" in words would be:

Satisfaction with time in queue = B0 + B1 (actual time in queue)

Using data that has been transformed to a 1 to 5 scale, and inserting the example results we would get: 69 = 92.27 + -1.3 (17.9), where 69 is the average rating of "satisfaction with queue time" (y), and 17.9 seconds (X) is the average actual "time in queue." The B1 (Beta) is negative so the relationship is negative.

Interpretation

If the "time in queue" where reduced by 1 unit (say one second) then the "satisfaction with the time in queue" would increase by 1.3 units (from 69 to 70.3). If the "time in queue" were reduced by 2 seconds, the "satisfaction" would increase by 2.6 units to 71.6. Therefore, reductions in actual "queue time" are predicted to increase perceptions of "satisfaction" in a dependable relationship of 1:1.3.

Case Study Two

Situation

In this example the variables are actual "talk time" versus "satisfaction with the length of the call." For the independent (X) variable "talk time," the equation in words would be:

Satisfaction with talk time = B0 + B1 (actual talk time)

Using data that has been transformed to a 1 to 5 scale, and inserting in the example results: 70 = -6.5 + .17 (450), where 70 is the average rating for "talk time satisfaction" and 450 seconds is the average "talk time" taken from the ACD output.

Interpretation

If the "talk time" was increased by 1 unit (i.e., 1 second) then "satisfaction with talk time" would increase by 0.17 units (from 70 to 70.17). If the "talk time" were increased by 2 seconds, the "satisfaction" would increase by $.17 \times 2 = .34$, so the ratio is 1:0.17.

Note that of the two examples, the second one has a much smaller improvement per unit of change (1:1.3 compared to 1:0.17) between the two independent variables. Looking strictly at these two ratios, it is obvious that talk times should be allowed to increase. But before such a decision can be rationally made, it is important to compute the costs of making changes. It may be that reducing queue time would require system changes that are prohibitively expensive this year, but can be accommodated next year, whereas hiring additional agents and encouraging everyone not to rush callers would be possible this year.

In addition to costs, statistical significance (or impact) needs to be assessed. (See Chapter 4 for discussion and examples). It does no good to make changes that cost only a little money if those changes will not substantially impact your customer satisfaction performance. Better to save the money to use on changes that will substantially impact customer satisfaction.

In conclusion, keep in mind that your focus must be on moving customer satisfaction into the customer delight range, which means achieving a CSI score of 85 or more. As should be clear now, multiple regression and other statistical techniques cannot make managerial decisions: costs, political and other organizational realities, and intuition all play an important part in executive decision-making.

Appendix H: The Importance of Corporate Image

Corporate Image versus Financial Performance

A company's contact center can have a major impact on corporate image. The frequently asked question "Does the public image of a corporation effect the volume of sales of its products or services?" was put to the test in a research conducted at Purdue University's Center for Customer-Driven Quality.

Although the research is still ongoing, initial results reported that in 80% of the Fortune 500 companies studied, the qualitative measure of image is a statistically significant leading indicator of direction of the next year's sales volume. All of the corporate image and sales volume data for the research was taken from *Fortune Magazine* over a period of ten years.

The specific question posed in the Purdue research can best be stated as follows:

"Does an increase or decrease in a company's public image this year have a corresponding increase or decrease in sales volume in the next year or years?"

Quantifying Annual Public Image

Since 1983, Fortune Magazine has published an annual list called "America's Most Admired Companies." Industry experts score their perception of each company on a qualitative scale from zero to five, where 0 = poor, and 5 = excellent. The companies are judged on eight key attributes of image that impact corporate reputation:

1. Quality of management
2. Quality of products or services
3. Quality of innovation
4. Quality of the company's value as a long-term investment
5. Quality of financial soundness
6. Quality of the work place as seen in the company's ability to attract, develop, and keep talented people
7. Quality of the company's community and environmental actions
8. Quality of the company's planned use of corporate assets

Quantifying the Annual Sales Volume

Fortune Magazine annually publishes the financial data on the "Fortune Top Five Hundred American Companies." This issue contains information for each company including annual sales volume, profits, return on equity, and many other important financial indicators of performance. From this data, the researchers studied the annual sales volume of each selected company.

Results and Conclusions

The results show that over a period of time the change in public image of a company is a statistically significant indicator of the *direction of change* in a company's sales volume, i.e., customers apparently prefer to purchase from companies whose image they admire. The results do not indicate any consistent relationship in the *magnitude* of the changes, just the direction; i.e., if image is up (or down) this year, sales volume is highly likely to be up (or down) next year.

By closely monitoring customer satisfaction and public image, company executives can get an early warning, i.e., a "wake-up call," that next year's sales volumes are going to be impacted by negative word-of-mouth. With this early warning system in place, every possible action should be taken to turn around the situation before the decrease in sales volume occurs with its possible negative effects on profits.

Approximately 20% of the companies studied did not conform to the findings reported, and therefore ongoing research is being conducted to determine what other factors might have influenced these companies to behave differently, i.e., mergers and acquisitions, or new product release that might impact sales volumes.

In conclusion, since corporate image has a high probability of impacting next year's revenue, a world-class contact center can be a major asset for companies.

APPENDIX I: CONTACT CENTER PERFORMANCE BENCHMARKING

Introduction to Performance Comparisons

As discussed in Chapter 3, the contact center is an environment full of data ready to be used for performance measurement and management. In this Appendix we have organized the measurements in groups most useful for measuring different types of performance. In the end, each contact center manager must select from these measurements those that may be most useful and applicable to managing a particular contact center with a specific set of corporate goals.

Contact Center Performance Measurements

- Service Level
- Average Speed of Answer
- Average Time in Queue
- Average Talk Time
- Average Auxiliary Time
- Average After-Call Work Time
- Average Handle Time
- Adherence to Schedule
- Average Abandonment Rate
- Average Time to Abandon
- Retrial Rate
- Agent Utilization
- Average Offered Call Volume Per Hour
- Average Handled Call Volume Per Hour
- Average Blocking Rate
- Revenue-Related Performance Measurements
- Percentage of Time Agents Spend on Calls
- Average Call Value
- Conversion Ratio of Inquiry Calls to Sales
- Average Sales per Agent
- Cost-Related Performance Measurements

- Loaded Cost per Agent
- Average Recruitment Cost
- Average Training Cost
- Average Training Time
- Average Cost per Call
- Average Cost per Order
- Ratio of IVR to Agent-Handled Calls
- Lawsuits Avoided
- Quality of Service Performance Measurements
- Average Tenure of Agents
- Overall Customer satisfaction
- Number of Complaints or Escalated Calls
- Percent of Calls Requiring Rework
- Complaints Resolved on First Call
- Agent Satisfaction
- Number of Transfers before Resolution

Contact Center Benchmarking

A "benchmark" is a standard of performance or a point of reference from which you can make other measurements. Contact centers lend themselves particularly well to benchmarking because so many elements of a contact center are measured. In fact, it would be fair to say that the company's contact center performance is undoubtedly the most measurable as seen by the many metrics discussed and defined in this book.

In contact centers, benchmarking may take many forms as described below:

1. Against the average of many contact centers in various industries

2. Against the average of many contact centers in the same industry

3. Against the best contact center in various industries

4. Against direct competitors in the same industry

Benchmarking Questionnaire for Customer Service
Call Centers

Purdue University
Center for Customer-Driven Quality

In-depth RealityCheck™ Survey

for

Inbound Customer Service Call Centers

Thank you for participating in our research into call center best practices.

In addition to this Survey, we also have in-depth RealityCheck™ Surveys for the following types of centers:

- Outbound Telemarketing
- Outbound Collections
- Inbound Technical Support to External Customers
- Inbound Technical Support to Internal Customers (Help Desk)
- E-mail Handling
- Web-chat Handling
- IVR Call Handling

Please make note of the following regarding this Survey:

1. An inbound call center is defined as any group of telephone Agents whose calls are distributed by an automatic call distributor (ACD) to the next available Agent.

2. Please use one questionnaire for each call center in your company.

3. Your individual performance data will be kept in strict confidence on our secured server.

4. When you have completed this Survey, you may submit your data by one of the following methods:

   - FAX your completed Survey to: (509) 351- 0264, or
   - MAIL your completed Survey to:

     BenchmarkPortal, Inc.
     RealityCheck™ Support
     3201 Airpark Drive, Suite 104
     Santa Maria, CA 93455

187

GR33-011105

Participant Information

Name _____

Title _____

E-mail Address _____

Company Name _____

Mailing Address_____

City _____ **State** _____ **Zip Code** _____

Phone Number _____ **Extension**_____

FAX Number _____

Toll-Free Number of Your Call Center_____

Referred by:_____ _____

If you have a problem completing your questionnaire, or you have any questions concerning benchmarking, please e-mail the RealityCheck[TM] Survey Team at:

Inbound.Customer.Service@BenchmarkPortal.com

From the Industry Groups Below, Please Circle One
Industry that Best Represents Your Company

Banking/Finance:
Banking
Brokerage
Credit Card
Mortgage
Other

Consumer Products:
Electronics
Food/Beverage
Health/Beauty
Pet supplies
Other

Government:
Federal
Municipal
State

Healthcare/Pharmaceutical:
Healthcare Provider
Pharmaceuticals
Other

Information Technology:
Computer Hardware
Computer Software
Other

Insurance:
Health
Life
Property/Casualty
Other

Manufacturing/Chemicals/
Construction:
Aerospace
Automotive
Building Materials/ Construction
Chemicals
Other

Media:
Radio
Publishing
Television
Other

Retail/Catalog:
Catalog
Online
Retail Store
Other

Transportation:
Public Transportation Systems
Rail
Toll Road
Trucking

Telecommunications:
- Cable/Broadband/Satellite
- Voice
- Data/Internet Service Provider
- Wireless
- Other

Travel:
- Airline
- Hotel/Resort/Cruise Line
- Travel Agency
- Other

Utilities/Fuel:
- Gas
- Electric
- Fuel Oil

Other: (Please specify) _____

Call Center Profile for Peer Group Classification

1. How many inbound calls per year are directed to your call center?

    Calls offered annually _____

    (Calls offered is the total number of calls you receive in a given year. This number is provided by your ACD.)

2. Of the inbound calls directed to your call center, how many are handled by a live Agent and/or your IVR?

    Calls handled annually _____
    (Calls handled are the number of calls you actually completed by a live Agent, plus calls handled by your IVR. Calls handled must be equal to, or less than calls offered.) This number is provided by your ACD.

3. Of all the calls handled annually by your center, how do they breakdown into the following two categories?

    Annual call volume handled by your Agents _____

    Annual call volume handled completely by your IVR _____

    ("Completely by your IVR" means that the call did not require a live Agent to complete the call and therefore, it was handled by caller "self service.")

4. Of the calls handled annually by your Agents, how do they breakdown in the following two categories?

    Business to business _____%
    (Fill in the percentage of calls handled that came from a business customer.)

    Business to consumer _____%
    (Fill in the percentage of calls handled that came from an individual consumer, also known as an "end user.")

    Total **100 %**

5. How many minutes of telephone usage are recorded annually by your call center's automatic call distributor (ACD)?

Annual

minutes   _____

6. How many Agents work at your call center?

   Full-time Agents   _____
   (Fill in the number of full-time Agents employed in your call center.)

   Part-time Agents   _____
   (Fill in the number of part-time Agents employed in your call center.)

7. How many Full Time Equivalent Agents (FTE) work at your call center?

   Full-time Equivalents (FTEs)   _____
   (FTE= Total Agent payroll hours per week divided by 40. A full-time Agent equals 1.0 FTE's. A part-time Agent who works 20 hours a week (half that of a full-time Agent) equals 0.5 FTE.)

8. Are your Agents represented by a labor union?

   ☐ Yes
   ☐ No

9. If your Agents do more than just answer inbound calls, what other functions do they perform?

<u>Agent Functions</u>	<u>Average Percent of Agent Time</u>
Inbound Calls	_____
Outbound Call	_____
Respond to E-mails	_____
Answer On-line Web-chats	_____
Other *If other, please specify:*	_____

   _____

10. Which of the following types of calls do your
Agents handle as a percent of their
total calls handled?

a. Customer Service   _____%
*(Providing callers with quick and accurate
answers to their questions, and/or logging and
updating customer information.)*

b. Order Taking and Order Tracking   _____%
*(Taking and tracking orders for products and/or
services.)*

c. Technical Support to External Customers   _____%
*(Handling product-use questions and "fix-it" questions
for external customers (if the percentage of support
calls is over 50%, you should complete our Technical
Support Survey, not this one.))*

d. Complaints   _____%
(Handling customer complaints.)

e. Re-directing Inbound Calls   _____%
(Routing callers to next available specialist.)

f. Other   _____%
*(Fill in the percentage of calls handled that are a
type other than any of the options provided
above.)*

If other, please describe:

_____

                                        Total   100 %

194

Call Center Costs

11. What is the total annual budget for your call center for this year?
(Fill in the annual operating budget allocated for your call center for this year.)

$_____

12. How do you compensate your Agents?
(Average hourly wage for front-line Agents.)

$_____

13. What is your average cost per call in dollars?
(This is the sum of all costs for running the call center for the period, divided by the number of calls handled in the call center for the same period. This would include all calls whether handled by an Agent or by the IVR.)

$_____

Call Center Performance Measures

14. Over the past 90 days, what were your average inbound performance time-based metrics?

a. 80% of your calls are answered in how many seconds
(This is (the number of calls answered in X seconds) divided by (offered calls) times 100.)
_____

b. Average speed of answer in seconds_____
(This is the total queue time, divided by the number of calls handled. This includes both IVR-handled calls as well as calls handled by a live Agent.)

c. Average talk time in minutes (includes hold time)
_____
(This is the average amount of time an Agent spends talking with a customer during the course of one phone call.)

d. Average after call work time in minutes_____
(This is the average amount of time an Agent spends on performing follow-up work after the Agent has disconnected from the caller.)

e. Average time in queue in seconds _____
(This is the average wait time that a caller endures. This differs from average speed of answer because this calculation includes only calls that actually had a

wait time. This metric is also known as average time of delay.)

f. Average time before abandoning in seconds_____
(This is the average amount of time a customer will wait in queue before abandoning.)

15. Over the past 90 days, what were your average inbound performance percentage-based metrics?

a. Average abandoned in percent_____
(This is the percentage of calls that get connected to the ACD, but get disconnected by the caller before reaching an Agent, or before completing a process within the IVR.)

b. Calls resolved on first call in percent_____
(This is the percentage of calls that were completely resolved during the course of the first inbound call initiated by the customer, and therefore do not require a call back.)

c. Calls blocked in percent_____
(These are calls that never make it to your ACD. Examples of blocked calls are: "busy signals," "number not in service" messages, etc. This number can be provided only by your telecommunications provider.)

d. Agent occupancy in percent_____
(This is the percentage of time that an Agent is in their seat connected to the ACD, and either engaged in a call or ready to answer a call as compared to the total number of hours at work.)

e. Adherence to schedule in percent_____
(This percentage represents how closely an Agent adheres to his/her detailed work schedule as provided by the workforce management system. 100% adherence means that the Agent was exactly where they were supposed to be at the time projected in their schedule. The scheduled time allows for meetings with the supervisor, education, plus answering customer phone calls.)

f. Average attendance in percent_____
(This is a percentage representing how often an Agent is NOT absent from work due to an unplanned absence (not to include excused absences, i.e., vacation, FMLA, jury duty, etc.). Take the total number of unexcused absences and divide it by the

196

total number of days that the Agent was expected to be at work, and subtract that number from 100.)

g. Average calls transferred in percent _____
(This represents the percent of calls transferred from the original Agent that connects with the customer.)

h. Average caller hold time in seconds while on the phone with an Agent
(This is the average amount of time, in seconds, that callers are on hold after being connected to an Agent. Most ACD systems provide this number.)

i. Average Auxiliary (Aux) Time in percent_____
(This is the average amount of time per shift, in percent, that an Agent is logged into an Aux state. This should include all authorized off-line time, i.e. time set aside for handling emails, training, or other job-related tasks.)

j. Average Utilization in percent_____
(Agent utilization is the percentage of time that an Agent is in their seat ready to handle calls as compared to the actual time they are in telephone mode. Utilization equals the product of average call handle time (talk time + hold time + after call work time) and the average number of inbound calls per Agent per 8-hour shift (ACPS), divided by total time the Agent is connected to the ACD and ready to handle calls during a shift, i.e., occupancy (not in percent).)

$$Utilization = \frac{(ATT + ACW)(ACPS)}{Occupancy} X100$$

16. How many inbound calls per hour are handled by your Agents?
(This is the average number of calls that an Agent handles per hour.)

_____

17. Does your call center have a formal process to collect the caller's satisfaction regarding their experience with how their call was handled?

☐ Yes
☐ No

18. On average, in the past 90 days what percentage of your callers gave you a

perfect score on the question, "Overall, how satisfied were you with the service you received during your call to our center?"

(a "highest" score of 5 out of 5, or the top of whatever scale you use)

_____%

19. On average, in the past 90 days, what percentage of your callers gave you the lowest score on the question, "Overall, how satisfied were you with the service you received during your call to our company?"

(a "lowest" score of 1 out of 5, or the top of whatever scale you use)

_____%

20. Does your call center have a formal mechanism for gathering Agent feedback?

(Does your call center gather both positive and/or negative feedback from your Agents?)

☐ Yes
☐ No

21. On average, in the past 90 days, what percentage of your Agents gave you a perfect score on the question, "Overall, how satisfied are you with your position?"

(a "highest" score of 5 out of 5, or the top of whatever scale you use)

_____%

22. On average, in the past 90 days, what percentage of your Agents gave you the lowest score on the question, "Overall, how satisfied are you with your position?"

(a "lowest" score of 1 out of 5, or the bottom of whatever scale you use)

_____%

23. What is the ratio of agents to supervisors (span of control)?

Agents per supervisor _____
(Fill in how many Agents, on average, you have assigned to each supervisor.)

24. What is the annual percentage turnover of your full-time Agents?

_____

25. As a percentage of total turnover (Question 24 above), how does this breakdown into the following two categories?

Promotional turnover _____
(This is the turnover caused by promotions within the call center from Agent to some other position in the call center, and/or promotions where Agents go to other departments within the company.)

All Other Turnover _____
(This is all other turnover not related to promotions, but related to and including voluntary and involuntary termination.)

26. Of your calls handled by the IVR, what percent of callers opt out to a live Agent?

_____%

Benchmarking Questionnaire for Inbound E-mail Contact Centers

Purdue University
Center for Customer-Driven Quality

E-mail Benchmark Questionnaire

Thank you for participating in our research into contact center performance levels. Please make note of the following:

Please use one questionnaire for each customer contact facility.

A contact center handles e-mails, and/or telephone calls (inbound or outbound), and/or Web site requests.

Your individual performance data will be kept in strict confidence on our secured server.

You will receive a free executive summary report comparing your performance against others in the database. This report will be sent to you by e-mail within approximately two to three weeks from the time you complete entering all of your data.

When you have completed your questionnaire, you may submit your data by one of the following methods:

Visit our Web site at www.BenchmarkPortal.com, create a new account or login to your existing account, and enter the questionnaire data online

FAX your completed survey to (805) 614-0055 for entry into the database

MAIL your completed survey to:

BenchmarkPortal, Inc.
3201 Airpark Drive, Suite 104
Santa Maria, CA 93455

```

```

Participant Account Information
(Required for FAX or mail questionnaire submissions)

*Name*_____

E-mail Address _____

Company Name _____

Mailing Address _____

City _____ **State** _____ **Zip Code** _____

Phone Number _____ **Ext.** _____

FAX Number _____

Company Web site _____

Contact Center E-mail Address _____

Classification

1. What is your total e-mail volume per month (exclusive of internal e-mail)?

Inbound e-mail volume per month   _____

Outbound e-mail volume per month   _____

2. What percentage of your total e-mail volume is secured?

☐ Between 0 - 25%

☐ Between 26 - 50%

☐ Between 51 - 75%

☐ Between 76 - 100%

☐ Don't use secured

3. Which of the following functions do your Agents provide regarding e-mail contacts?

Buying / bidding	_____ %
Selling / listing	_____ %
Registration	_____ %
Customer service (questions and inquiries)	_____ %
Technical support – external	_____ %
Site issues	_____ %
Order taking and tracking	_____ %
Information requests	_____ %
Public relations	_____ %
Complaint resolution	_____ %
Other	_____ %
Total	**100 %**

4. How do your inbound e-mails break down in the following categories:

Business to business	_____ %
Business to consumer	_____ %
Consumer to consumer	_____ %
Total	**100 %**

5. Do you use an automatic e-mail response system at your contact center?

☐ Yes
☐ No

6. How many Agents work at your contact center?

Full-time Agents   _____

Part-time Agents   _____

Contract Agents   _____

Full-time Equivalents (FTEs)

(FTE = Total payroll hours per week divided by 40 hours per week)

Customer Contact Center Costs

7. What is the total annual budget for your contact center?
(Include everything that is mentioned in the next question.)

Last year	$_____
This year	$_____
Next year	$_____

8. What percentage of your ongoing cost is for:

Human Resources - salary, benefits, etc.	_____%
Human Resources - recruiting, screening, training	_____%
Telecommunications Line Charge	_____%
Computer Hardware	_____%
Computer Software	_____%
Telecommunications Equipment	_____%
Real Estate (floor space)	_____%
Outsourced contracts	_____%
Other	_____%
Total	**100 %**

9. What is your fully loaded cost per e-mail in dollars?

Cost per e-mail in dollars $_____

10. What percentage of your annual revenue is your fully loaded annual e-mail cost?

_____%

Performance Measurement

11. What percentage of e-mail contacts are answered in how many hours?

Less than 2 hours	_____ %
Between 2 - 4 hours	_____ %
Between 4 - 6 hours	_____ %
Between 6 - 8 hours	_____ %
Between 8 - 12 hours	_____ %
Between 12 - 24 hours	_____ %
Between 24 - 36 hours	_____ %
Greater than 36 hours	_____ %
Total	**100 %**

12. What is your service level goal for e-mail response? (percentage handled in how many hours)

Within 2 hours	_____ %
Within 4 hours	_____ %
Within 6 hours	_____ %
Within 8 hours	_____ %
Within 12 hours	_____ %
Within 24 hours	_____ %
Within 36 hours	_____ %

13. What are your inbound e-mail service level statistics?

Average Agent time per e-mail in minutes	_____minutes
Contacts resolved on first e-mail response in percent	_____%
Average number of e-mail contacts per resolution	_____
Agent occupancy in percent	_____%
Adherence to schedule in percent	_____%
Average attendance in percent	_____%
Cost per contact transaction in dollars	$_____
Average sale value in dollars	$_____
Average e-mail contacts handled per hour per Agent	_____
Average e-mail contacts handled per 8-hour shift per Agent	_____

Performance Measurement

14. What percentage of your e-mail volume is repeat e-mail to the same customer trying to solve the same problem or answer the same question?

Percentage of re-sent e-mails _____%

15. What is your e-mail error rate (number of errors per 1000 e-mails)?

(An error is a mistake or action that requires human intervention to correct.)

Errors per 1000 e-mails _____

16. Does your contact center do any up-selling/cross-selling?

☐ Yes
☐ No

17. What percentage of contacts give rise to up-selling/cross-selling opportunities?

_____%

18. What is your average sale value per up-sell/cross-sell in dollars?

$_____

19. What is the primary indicator of your e-mail associates' productivity?

☐ E-mail responses per hour
☐ E-mail responses per shift
☐ Average processing time per response
☐ Do not measure associates' e-mail productivity
☐ Other

20. Please specify the "other" indicator of your e-mail associates' productivity:

_____

Satisfaction Measurement

21. Does your contact center have a formal mechanism for gathering customer feedback on contact center performance?

☐ Yes
☐ No

22. What percentage of your customer contacts gives you a percent score?
   (e.g., a perfect score of 5 out of 5, or a perfect score of 7 out of 7)

   _____%

23. What percentage of contacts to the center result in a complaint about how a previous e-mail was handled?

   _____%

Human Resource Management

24. What percentage of Agents work at each level in your contact center?

Level one _____%

Level two _____%

Level three _____%

Level four and higher _____%

25. If more than four levels of Agents work in your contact center, please specify the number of levels?

_____

26. What is the ratio of Agents to supervisors (span of control)?

Agents per supervisor _____

27. What is the annual turnover of your inbound Agent staff? *(including both internal transfers and external attrition)*

Full-time _____%

Part-time _____%

28. How do you compensate your Agents?

Base salary per year only $_____

Per hour only $_____

29. What is the average annual salary of your supervisors?

$_____

30. What is the average annual salary of your contact center manager?

$_____

31. What is the length (in hours) of your initial, new-hire training period for Agents?

_____hours

32. How much does it cost you to bring on a new Agent (including recruiting, screening, training)?

New Agent hiring cost in dollars $_____

33. Do you have a specific hiring/selection process for an
     associate's e-mail related skills?

☐ Yes
☐ No
☐ Don't know

Human Resource Management

34. Are your Agents represented by a labor union?

☐ Yes

☐ No

35. What percentage of your total contact volume is handled by part-time Agents?

_____%

Process & Knowledge

36. Of your customer service e-mail messages, what percentage are:

Automatically routed to the appropriate Agent from Web site _____%

Automatically routed to the appropriate Agent from e-mail system (non-Web form e-mail) _____%

Manually routed to the appropriate Agent _____%

37. Is the software application you use to process e-mail messages:

☐ Proprietary
☐ Commercial

38. If a commercial software application is used to process e-mail messages, what vendor do you use?

_____

39. Of your automated responses, what percentage of your e-mail messages are serviced using:

Templates	_____%
Form letters	_____%
Form paragraphs	_____%
Free-form responses	_____%
Auto-acknowledge	_____%
Auto-suggest	_____%
Auto-response	_____%
Other	_____%
Total	**100 %**

40. What is your average e-mail turnover time per response?

Turnaround in hours _____hours

41. What percentage of e-mail responses are undeliverable?

_____%

42. What are your hours of operation for handling e-mail messages?

Number of hours per weekday, Monday through Friday   _____

Number of hours per Saturday   _____

Number of hours per Sunday   _____

Number of hours per Holiday   _____

43. On average, what percentage of your e-mail associates' time is spent performing some other function?

☐ Between 0 - 25%

☐ Between 26 - 50%

☐ Between 51 - 75%

☐ Between 76 - 100%

☐ E-mail associates do not perform other functions

44. Is the contact center integrated with other customer access touchpoints?

(for instance, phone, Web site, FAX-back, kiosk)

☐   Yes

☐ _____ *No*

45. On the Internet, which alternate touchpoints does your Web site offer?

(check all that apply)

☐ Your contact center's 1-800 number

☐ A self-service option (e.g., a static FAQ section)

☐ Voice Over IP, or Internet contact

☐ Instant Messaging (chat capabilities)

☐ Discussion boards, voice groups, etc.

46. Of all your inbound contacts, what percentage is handled by self-service?

_____ %

Quality Management

47. How do you measure quality?*(check all that apply)*
☐ By sampling
☐ Number of e-mails required to solve one customer request
☐ Error rate per associate
☐ Error rate per 1000 responses for center
☐ We do not measure quality
☐ We use an external company to measure quality
☐ Other

48. Please specify the name of the external company used to measure quality:

_____

49. How often do you measure the quality of each associate's e-mail responses (excluding escalations)?
☐ Daily
☐ Weekly
☐ Bi-weekly
☐ Monthly
☐ Quarterly
☐ Other

50. How often do you review the quality of each Agent's e-mail responses with the Agent (excluding escalations)?
☐ Daily
☐ Weekly
☐ Bi-weekly
☐ Monthly
☐ Quarterly
☐ Other

Outsourcing

51. Does your center outsource any contacts or functions?

☐ Yes
☐ No

52. What percentage of your total contacts do you outsource?

_____%

Facilities and Design

53. What is the total number of Agent workstations at your
       contact center?

Seats   _____

54. What percentage of your workstations are used by more than
       one Agent per day (desk sharing)?

                                                            _____%

55. How large is your average Agent cubical workspace?

Square feet   _____

56. How many total square feet does your contact center occupy?

Square feet   _____

Additional Metrics

57. Are there additional metrics and/or key performance
    indicators that you would like to have included in this
    ☐   questionnaire?
    Yes
    ☐ No

58. Please enter additional metric or key performance indicator
    you would like to have included in this questionnaire:

_____

59. Please enter additional metric or key performance indicator
    you would like to have included in this questionnaire:

_____

60. Please enter additional metric or key performance indicator
    you would like to have included in this questionnaire:

_____

APPENDIX J: COMPLAINT MANAGEMENT CHECKLIST

In planning a system for complaint management or evaluating the one you have in place, consider the following questions:

- Does your company view consumer satisfaction as a key ingredient of total quality management?
- Do you have a systematic strategy for complaint management?
- Do you have written procedures for your complaint management system?
- Is staff throughout the company well aware of the procedures and the importance of your complaint management system?
- Does top management directly oversee your complaint handling procedures?
- Do incentives exist to reinforce staff commitment to consumer satisfaction?
- Is your complaint system easily accessible to consumers?
- Is your complaint system computerized?
- Have you considered a toll-free number for complaints and inquiries?
- Do you publicize your complaint system to consumers? If yes, how? Printed media (posters, advertising, monthly statements, on packaging, labeling, and products)?
- Communications by sales personnel?
- Is your complaint system:
    - decentralized, with each employee, branch office, or store responsible for resolving complaints?
    - centralized in one department or location?

- o   or a combination of both, with larger or more serious complaints resolved in a central office?
- Are you providing adequate training for your complaint management staff?
- Does the customer relations staff feel they have equal stature with other professionals in the company?
- Do you periodically survey your customers to see if they are satisfied with your complaint management system? Do you encourage feedback?
- Do you regularly review your complaint management system and make necessary improvements?
- Do you utilize your system of complaint management for more than settling individual complaints? For example, for quality control and problem prevention?
- Does your complaint system swiftly generate systematic information about causes of complaints and complaint trends? Does this data meet your management needs?
- Do you circulate to top management periodic reports of data from complaint records with suggestions for action to prevent recurring problems?
- Can you identify areas in the company where your complaint management system is having an effect? Has it been positive or negative?
- Do you coordinate your complaint management system with others in the distribution chain for your products or services? Do you have a direct line of communication with them?
- Do you have an adequate understanding of how these external organizations are affecting your relationship with customers?
- Do you work cooperatively with governmental consumer agencies?
- Do you use third-party dispute settlement mechanisms for those problems not resolved in-house?
- Has the use of third-party or in-house mechanisms had any effect on the number of regulatory actions (both private and governmental) involving your company?

APPENDIX K: ADDITIONAL SOURCES OF GUIDANCE AND ASSISTANCE IN MANAGING COMPLAINTS

For help in developing your company's complaint management procedures and information about third-party systems, contact your industry trade association You may also contact:

Council of Better Business Bureaus
4200 Wilson Boulevard, Suite 800
Arlington, VA 22203
(703) 276-0100

American Arbitration Association
140 West 51st Street
New York, NY 10020-1203
(212) 484-4000

Federal Trade Commission
Division of Marketing Practices
Washington, DC 20580
(202) 326-3128

Society of Consumer Affairs Professionals in Business
801 North Fairfax Street, Suite 404
Alexandria, VA 22314
(703) 519-3700

National Association of Consumer Agency Administrators
1010 Vermont Avenue, N.W., Suite 514
Washington, DC 20005
(202) 347-7395

National Coalition for Consumer Education
434 Main Street, Suite 201
Chatham, NJ 07928
(201) 635-1916

National Institute for Dispute Resolution
1901 L Street, N.W., Suite 600
Washington, DC 22204
(202) 466-4764

ABOUT THE SPONSOR

UCN is the leading provider of all-in-one, off-premises contact handling services that improve the customer contact experience and the productivity of those handling the contacts. InContact® includes an integrated suite of core contact handling applications, including contact routing, interactive menus, database integration, automated surveys and scoring analysis, reporting, monitoring, recording, administration and workforce scheduling and forecasting applications. InControl™ is a unique, drag-and-drop application development tool that enables inContact customers to build highly flexible, customized contact handling processes that can be setup and changed in hours or minutes compared to weeks or months that are common with premises-based contact center software and equipment. InContact never becomes obsolete and does not require major upfront capital investments every three or four years. You can now enjoy the benefits of state-of-the-art for all major contact center software components, all of the time, across all of your locations.

UCN operates its own national IP network supporting traditional TDM as well as VoIP connectivity methods or blends of the two at your different locations. The hosted software offers built-in disaster recovery with fully redundant data centers in Los Angeles and Dallas with network connectivity into all of the major carriers with real-time failover backed by an enterprise-grade SLA for both network services and on-demand contact center applications. Emergency contact handling scripts can be pre-built and stored allowing fast cutover for rerouting calls to remote agents wherever they have access to a telephone and PC.